FALLEN LEAVES

ALSO BY WILL DURANT

The Story of Philosophy (1926)

Transition (1927)

The Mansions of Philosophy (1929)

The Case for India (1930)

Adventures in Genius (1931)

A Program for America (1931)

On the Meaning of Life (1932)

The Tragedy of Russia (1933)

The Story of Civilization—Vol. 1: Our Oriental Heritage (1935)

The Story of Civilization—Vol. II: The Life of Greece (1939)

The Story of Civilization—Vol. III: Caesar and Christ (1944)

The Story of Civilization—Vol. IV: The Age of Faith (1950)

The Story of Civilization—Vol. V: The Renaissance (1953)

The Story of Civilization—Vol. VI: The Reformation (1957)

The Story of Civilization—Vol. VII: The Age of Reason Begins
(1961)

The Story of Civilization—Vol. VIII: The Age of Louis XIV (1963)

The Story of Civilization—Vol. IX: The Age of Voltaire (1965)

The Story of Civilization—Vol. X: Rousseau and Revolution (1967)

The Lessons of History (1968)

Interpretations of Life (1970)

The Story of Civilization -- Vol. XI: The Age of Napoleon (1975)

A Dual Autobiography (1977)

Heroes of History (2001)

The Greatest Minds and Ideas of All Time (2002)

Heroes of Civilization (audio) (2014)

FALLEN LEAVES

LAST WORDS ON
Life, Love, War,
AND *God*

WILL
DURANT

Simon & Schuster Paperbacks

NEW YORK   LONDON   TORONTO   SYDNEY   NEW DELHI

Simon & Schuster Paperbacks
An Imprint of Simon & Schuster, Inc.
1230 Avenue of the Americas
New York, NY 10020

First Simon & Schuster trade paperback edition December 2015

SIMON & SCHUSTER PAPERBACKS and colophon are registered
trademarks of Simon & Schuster, Inc.

For information about special discounts for bulk purchases,
please contact Simon & Schuster Special Sales at 1-866-506-1949
or business@simonandschuster.com.

The Simon & Schuster Speakers Bureau can bring authors to your
live event. For more information or to book an event, contact the
Simon & Schuster Speakers Bureau at 1-866-248-3049 or visit
our website at www.simonspeakers.com.

Interior design by Akasha Archer

Manufactured in the United States of America

10 9 8 7 6

The Library of Congress has cataloged the hardcover edition as follows:

Durant, Will, 1885–1981.
  Fallen leaves : last words on life, love, war, and God / Will Durant. — First
Simon & Schuster hardcover edition.
     pages cm
  ISBN 978-1-4767-7154-0 (hardcover : alk. paper) — ISBN 978-1-4767-
7156-4 (ebook) — ISBN 978-1-4767-7155-7 (trade pbk. : alk. paper) 1.
Philosophy, American—20th century. I. Title.
  B934.D87 2014
  191—dc23
                                    2014021058
ISBN 978-1-4767-7154-0
ISBN 978-1-4767-7155-7 (pbk)
ISBN 978-1-4767-7156-4 (ebook)

CONTENTS

FALLEN LEAVES

FOREWORD

*I particularly am writing a book called "Fallen Leaves,"
expressing my feelings about the various writers of our time and
about the problems of our time.*

—WILL DURANT (TELEVISION INTERVIEW, JANUARY 1968)

*Durant is working on a new book, "Fallen Leaves"—"a not
very serious book which answers the questions of what I think
about government, life, death and God."*

—St. Petersburg Times, NOVEMBER 5, 1975

*Dr. Durant also is planning something tentatively entitled
"Fallen Leaves." "In which I propose—perhaps with Ariel's
help—to answer all the important questions—simply, fairly
and imperfectly," he said.*

—B.B.H. Independent, TUESDAY, NOVEMBER 6, 1975

*Durant is using his European vacation to finish up what he
describes as a little book of stray thoughts on everything. He
writes on a yellow legal pad whenever he has a moment and he
plans to finish the book before returning home to receive a joint
honorary degree with his wife next month. "I'm anxious to get
it done," said Durant. "The pep is petering out."*

—Los Angeles Times, MAY 26, 1978

That was it. A total of four aggravatingly brief statements about a book that no one, not even the Durant heirs, knew existed. And, unless you happened to live in Los Angeles, where the above television interview was aired in 1968 and two of the three newspaper articles were published during the mid- to late 1970s, you would not have known anything about Will Durant even contemplating the writing of such a book. Frustrating indeed.

It was considered to be Durant's most important work; the culmination of his sixty-plus years spent researching the philosophies, religions, arts, sciences, and civilizations of the world. It was to be the distilled wisdom and considered conclusions about our species' perennial problems and greatest joys, from a man who had not only read about life but had lived it through some of the world's most profound and cataclysmic moments—two world wars, the Great Depression, the rise of socialism and anarchism, the decline of religious belief, and the gradual change in American morals from the Victorian era to Woodstock. Durant had been born in 1885, when the primary mode of transportation between towns was the horse and carriage; he died in 1981—twelve years after man had first walked on the surface of the moon. What changes he had witnessed— and what interesting and often predictable cycles of human behavior! Certainly such patterns, particularly when viewed against the backdrop of human history, would be worth sharing for the benefit and education of future generations. What, for instance, was to be said for religious faith, after Darwin and science had toppled God from his throne in heaven and put nothing in his place but the gloomy angst of existentialists such as Jean-Paul Sartre? What is it in our nature that makes wars and conflict seemingly unavoidable? And what is the deeper meaning of life, love, and happiness? What is the purpose of art? Of science? What educational approach is best—and what makes man (or one man, at least) attracted to woman? Herein were to be the answers to such questions as only a thinker and writer of Durant's caliber could answer them. It was to be a message of insight for those who had sought meaning in life or the council of a learned friend in navigating life's journey. And it was also believed to be a manuscript that had inexplicably been "lost."

I had only learned of the manuscript after I had undertaken the move of the Durant archive to my home in Ontario, Canada. And then it had been as a result of several months poring over newspaper clippings, old essays, letters, audio recordings, decaying movie film, magazine articles, and cryptic jottings that became the fodder for certain volumes of The Story of Civilization. There were of course many delightful surprises during this period; chiefly the discovery of Dr. Durant's manuscript for *Heroes of History* and the audio recordings that he created with his wife, Ariel, for that project (both written and recorded during his ninety-third year). Evidently Durant had still been working on *Fallen Leaves* in some capacity during this period. But then after happening upon the tantalizing fragments given above there was nothing, no scrap of paper even indicating such a title, no evidence at all that such a manuscript ever existed. As the Durant archive had been well picked over by manuscript houses shortly after his passing, I knew that I hadn't seen absolutely everything he had written. I contacted his granddaughter, Monica Mihell, about getting in touch with these archive houses to at least see what they had in inventory from the Durant papers. Some were cooperative; others would not return calls.

And then I happened upon an archive house that indicated that they had sent the Durant estate copies of their collection, which included letters between Will and Ariel and a manuscript entitled *Fallen Leaves*! An extensive search of the Durant archive by both Monica and myself, along with repeated attempts to obtain an additional copy from the archive house—or even a contact for the person who might have this treasure in his possession—proved fruitless. The archive house indicated that they had given the estate photocopies of what they had shortly after their purchase and that was all that they were prepared to do.

And then Monica sold her house. During the course of packing, she came upon a box marked DURANT COPIES and, lo and behold, inside were not only some 2,100 papers of correspondence between Will and Ariel Durant (itself fascinating and most certainly print-worthy; indeed, certain of the letters the Durants had published themselves in their 1977 offering *A Dual Autobiography*), but also various drafts of the manuscript for *Fallen Leaves*. What was lost had now been found and could be made known. The result is the book you are holding in your hands—the final unpublished work of Will Durant.

Fallen Leaves is, perhaps, Will Durant's most personal book, presenting Durant's own opinions (rather than those of others, such as statesmen and eminent philosophers) on the major problems of life, politics, religion, and society. It is, at least in one respect, an ideal tome, as who among us has at one time or another not wished to seek the counsel of one wiser than ourselves? And who better to ask advice from about our most pressing concerns and social issues than a man who not only had lived long enough to have passed through all of the various hazardous straits of life, but who also was renowned for his broad erudition and knowledge of virtually all cultures and civilizations, and who had traveled the world several times over to better understand the ways of human behavior? In *Fallen Leaves* Durant's words are as insightful and revealing now as ever before; a joy to read (as his prose always is) and, unlike most philosophers who delight in obscurity, Durant's insights and recommendations are not only practical but easy for lay people to comprehend.

Gauging from the chapters, which were uncharacteristically all dated in Dr. Durant's hand, he began writing *Fallen Leaves* on March 20, 1967, roughly one year prior to the release of his book *The Lessons of History*, and coinciding with the release of *Interpretations of Life*. And, as he referenced the work in newspaper interviews well into the late 1970s, it appears that Durant had continued to work on the book for over a decade.

The concept had been for Durant to present his views on various social, religious, and political issues (this he did by revisiting and revising certain of his earlier and lesser-known writings on certain subjects and crafting entirely new material for others) and then to branch off into a survey of modern (twentieth-century) literature and philosophy. He had even completed one chapter into the second part of this enterprise when evidently he felt uncomfortable making such pronouncements without Ariel accompanying him. At this point, he involved her in the project and the second half of the book became so detailed and weighty that it became a book unto itself—and was published as such in 1970 under the title *Interpretations of Life*. It was a wise course, as it would have made for quite a leap going from one man's survey and interpretation of life to the varied books, art, and individual philosophies of twenty-six other novelists, poets, and philosophers. After the publication of *Interpretations of Life*, Durant returned to work on *Fallen Leaves* and would continue to do so until his death on November 7, 1981.

Durant's final years were inordinately prolific, as he not only continued his work on *Fallen Leaves*, but also found time to compose the book that would become *Heroes of History*, as well as to record his reading of this text in what would prove to be his final presentation of history as philosophy. *Fallen Leaves*, however, remained his pet project. While writing about history in his Story of Civilization series was what his public and publisher expected of him, to do so objectively required Durant to suppress his own ideas and beliefs in order to do justice to the thoughts of others—and one can only hold one's tongue on matters of great importance for so long. That Durant had managed to do so for over forty years is a quite a wonder in itself. As he mentions in his preface, he had over the years received letters from "curious readers who have challenged me to speak *my mind* on the timeless questions of human life and fate" (italics mine)—and he responded to their challenge with *Fallen Leaves*, spilling forth his views on such a wide range of topics—from sex to war, to the stages of life, to our minds and souls, to major social issues such as racism, the then ongoing war in Vietnam, the welfare state, and the problems and glories of both art and science.

Some reviewers may be critical of Durant's occasionally paternalistic discussion of women in this book. However, it must be remembered that, in keeping with the entire corpus of his work, Durant didn't stand outside of time but decidedly within it. Indeed, it is precisely because this is true that the observations he makes in *Fallen Leaves* are so resonant. They are the received wisdom of a man steeped in millennia of history, of which he was always aware that he was but a segment of its totality ("a drop of water attempting to analyze the sea," as he once said). Just as one must extrapolate from his chapter on Vietnam the broader historical insights that apply to a nation's power, ideology, and imperial ambition, however idealistic, so, too, must readers hear the recurring liberalism—a foundational faith in liberty and equality and their spread—in all of these chapters. Such a sentiment, I believe, will allow readers to enjoy the full measure of these chapters' wisdom without being drawn to any single statement or paragraph. Like the historical figures with whom Durant populated his and Ariel's opus, Durant himself has more than earned that benefit of contextualization.

Here, then, for posterity is the "lost" (and almost never known) and final manuscript of Will Durant. It contains strong opinions, elegant prose, and deep insights into the human condition, born of a lifetime of study of different cultures, arts, sciences, and human history—as only Will Durant could write it. To discover the last manuscript of a Pulitzer Prize–winning author such as Will Durant over thirty years after his passing is surely a major literary event, not only to fans of history and philosophy but to those who treasure dazzling and compelling prose. To such people, this book will surely have been worth the wait.

John Little

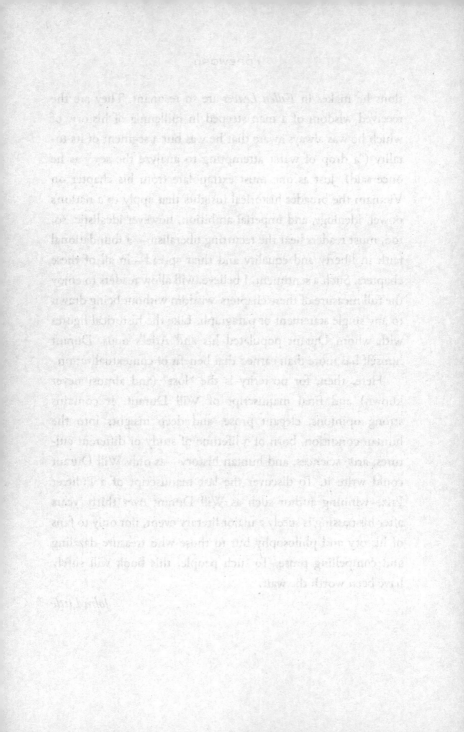

Vanity increases with age. Here I am, going on ninety-five; by this time I should have learned the art of silence, and should realize that every educated reader has already heard all opinions and their opposites; yet here I set out, fearful and rash, to tell the world—or one hundred millionth of it—just what I think on everything. It is all the more ridiculous since, at my age, a man is deeply rooted in the ways or views of his youth, and is almost constitutionally incapable of understanding the changing world that assails him, and from which he tends to flee into the grooves of the past or the safety of his home.

Why, then, should I write? I take as a vain excuse the letters of curious readers who have challenged me to speak my mind on the timeless questions of human life and fate. But in truth my chief reason for writing—aside from the narcissism implicit in all authorship—is that I find myself incapable of doing anything else with continuing interest. I propose to tell, in a very informal way, without the grandeur of obscurity, how I feel, now that I have one foot in the grave, about those ultimate riddles that I dealt with so recklessly some years ago in my books *Philosophy and the Social Problem* (1917), *The Story of Philosophy* (1926), *Transition* (1927), *The Mansions (or Pleasures) of Philosophy* (1929), and *On the Meaning of Life* (1932).

I know that life is in its basis a mystery; a river flowing from an unseen source and in its development an infinite subtlety; a "dome of many-colored glass," too complex for thought, much less for utterance.

And yet the thirst for unity draws me eternally on. To chart this wilderness of experience and history, to bring into focus the future, the unsteady light of the past, to bring into significance and purpose the chaos of sensation and desire, to discover the direction of life's majestic stream and thereby in some measure, perhaps, to control its flow: this insatiable metaphysical lust is one of the noble aspects of our questioning race. Our grasp is greater than our reach; but therefore our reach is made greater than that grasp.

So let us try, however vainly, to see human existence as a whole, from the moment when we are flung unasked into the world, until the wheel on which we are bound comes full circle in death. And as we pass through the ages of man's life— through childhood, youth, maturity, and old age—let us face the major problems of philosophy in metaphysics, ethics, politics, religion, and art, and make our little walk together a circumnavigation of the intellectual globe. It will subject us to inevitable superficiality, platitude, and error; but it may bring us just a trifle closer to the worth and meaning of our complex lives, and to that total perspective which is truth.

Please do not expect any new system of philosophy, nor any world-shaking cogitations; these will be human confessions, not divine revelations; they are micro- or mini-essays whose only dignity lies in their subjects rather than in their profundity or their size. If you find anything original here it will be unintentional, and probably regrettable. Knowledge grows, but wisdom, though it can improve with years, does not progress with centuries. I cannot instruct Solomon.

So, brave reader, you have fair warning: proceed at your own risk. But I shall be warmed by your company.

Will Durant

CHAPTER ONE

OUR LIFE BEGINS

A group of little children with their ways and chatter flow in,
Like welcome rippling water o'er my heated nerves and flesh.

—WALT WHITMAN, "AFTER THE ARGUMENT"

We like children first of all because they are ours; prolongations of our luscious and unprecedented selves. However, we also like them because they are what we would but cannot be—coordinated animals, whose simplicity and unity of action are spontaneous, whereas in the philosopher they come only after struggle and suppression. We like them because of what in us is called selfishness—the naturalness and undisguised directness of their instincts. We like their unhypocritical candor; they do not smile to us when they long for our annihilation. *Kinder und Narren sprechen die Wahrheit*—"Children and fools speak the truth"; and somehow they find happiness in their sincerity.

See him, the newborn, dirty but marvelous, ridiculous in

actuality, infinite in possibility, capable of that ultimate miracle—growth. Can you conceive it—that this queer bundle of sound and pain will come to know love, anxiety, prayer, suffering, creation, metaphysics, death? He cries; he has been so long asleep in the quiet warm womb of his mother; now suddenly he is compelled to breathe, and it hurts; compelled to see light, and it pierces him; compelled to hear noise, and it terrifies him. Cold strikes his skin, and he seems to be all pain. But it is not so; nature protects him against this initial onslaught of the world by dressing him in a general insensitivity. He sees the light only dimly; he hears the sounds as muffled and afar. For the most part he sleeps. His mother calls him a "little monkey," and she is right; until he walks he will be like an ape, and even less of a biped, the womb-life having given his funny little legs the incalculable flexibility of a frog's. Not till he talks will he leave the ape behind, and begin to climb precariously to the stature of a human being.

Watch him, and see how, bit by bit, he learns the nature of things by random movements of exploration. The world is a puzzle to him; and these haphazard responses of grasping, biting, and throwing are the pseudopodia, which he puts out to a perilous experience. Curiosity consumes and develops him; he would touch and taste everything from his rattle to the moon. For the rest he learns by imitation, though his parents *think* he learns by sermons. They teach him gentleness, and beat him; they teach him mildness of speech, and shout at him; they teach him a Stoic apathy to finance, and quarrel before him about the division of their income; they teach him honesty, and answer his most profound questions with lies. Our children bring us up by showing us, through imitation, what we really are.

The child might be the beginning and the end of philosophy. In its insistent curiosity and growth lies the secret of all metaphysics; looking upon it in its cradle, or as it creeps across the floor, we see life not as an abstraction, but as a flowing reality that breaks through all our mechanical categories, all our physical formulas. Here in this expansive urgency, this patient effort and construction, this resolute rise from hands to feet, from helplessness to power, from infancy to maturity, from wonder to wisdom—here is the "Unknowable" of Spencer, the *Noumenon* of Kant, the *Ens Realissimum* of the Scholastics, the "Prime Mover" of Aristotle, the *To ontos on*, or "That Which Really Is," of Plato; here we are nearer to the basis of things than in the length and breadth and thickness and weight and solidity of matter, or in the cogs and pulleys and wheels and levers of a machine. Life is that which is discontent, which struggles and seeks, which suffers and creates. No mechanistic or materialistic philosophy can do it justice, or understand the silent growth and majesty of a tree, or compass the longing and laughter of children.

Childhood may be defined as the age of play; therefore some children are never young, and some adults are never old.

CHAPTER TWO

ON YOUTH

Youth is the transition from play to work, from dependence on the family to dependence on one's self. It is a little anarchic and egotistic, because in the family its every whim or want was favored by unstinting parental love. Passing into the world, youth, petted for years and now for the first time free, drinks in the deep delight of liberty and advances to conquer and remold the universe.

Good oratory, said Demosthenes, is characterized by three points—action, action, and action, but he might have said it just as well of youth. Youth is as confident and improvident as a god. It loves excitement and adventure more than food. It loves the superlative, the exaggerated, the limitless, because it has abounding energy and frets to liberate its strength. It loves new and dangerous things; a man is as young as the risks he takes.

It bears law and order grudgingly. It is asked to be quiet when noise is the vital medium of youth; it is asked to be passive when it longs for action; it is asked to be sober and judicious when its very blood makes youth "a continuous intoxication." It is the age of abandon, and its motto, undelphianly, is *Panta agan*—"Everything in excess." It is never tired; it lives in the present, regrets no yesterdays, and dreads no morrows; it climbs buoyantly a hill whose summit conceals the other side. It is the age of sharp sensation and unchilled desire; experience is not soured yet with repetition and disillusionment; to have sensation at all is then a sweet and glorious thing. Every moment is loved for itself, and the world is accepted as an esthetic spectacle, something to be absorbed and enjoyed, something of which one may write verses, and for which one may thank the stars.

Happiness is the free play of the instincts, and so is youth. For the majority of us it is the only period of life in which we *live*; most men of forty are but a reminiscence, the burnt-out ashes of what was once a flame. The tragedy of life is that it gives us wisdom only when it has stolen youth. *Si jeunesse savait, et vieillesse pouvait!*—"If youth knew how, and old age could!"

Health lies in action, and so it graces youth. To be busy is the secret of grace, and half the secret of content. Let us ask the gods not for possessions, but for things to do; happiness is in making things rather than in consuming them. In Utopia, said Thoreau, each would build his own home; and then song would come back to the heart of man, as it comes to the bird when it builds its nest. If we cannot build our homes, we can at least walk and throw and run; and we should never be so old as merely to watch games instead of playing them. *Let us play* is as good as *Let us pray*, and the results are more assured.

Hence youth is wise in preferring the athletic field to the classroom, and in rating baseball above philosophy. Years ago, when a bespectacled Chinese student described American universities as "athletic associations in which certain opportunities for study are provided for the feeble-bodied," his remark was not so destructive as he supposed, and it described himself as much as the universities. Every philosopher, like Plato, should be an athlete; if he is not, let us suspect his philosophy.

"The first requisite of a gentleman," said Nietzsche, "is to be a perfect animal." On that foundation education should rise and build; instruction in the care of the body should equal the lore of the mind. The pangs of despised love and the bitterness of truth will not long torture a frame made sound and strong by sleep in the air and action in the sun.

Meanwhile youth is learning to read (which is all that one learns in school), and is learning where and how to find what he may later need to know (which is the best of the arts that he acquires in college). Nothing learned from a book is worth anything until it is used and verified in life; only then does it begin to affect behavior and desire. It is Life that educates, and perhaps love more than anything else in life.

For meanwhile puberty has come, and with it that self-consciousness which is the origin of thought. Suddenly the boy has lost the readiness and unity of indeliberate action and the pale cast of thought overshadows him. The girl begins to bedeck herself more carefully, to dishevel her hair more artfully; ten hours a day she thinks of dress, and a hundred times a day she draws her skirt down over her knees with charming futility. The boy begins to wash his neck and shine his shoes; half his income goes to the girl, the other half to the tailor. The girl learns the technique of blushing, and the young man, in the presence of beauty, walks "as if he had stolen his legs." Intellectual development comes step by step with the growing consciousness of sex. Instinct gives way to thought, action slips into quiet brooding.

There is a blossoming of poetry and imagination; a thousand fancies and magnificent ambitions flood the soul.

And at the same time that youth examines itself, it examines the world. It stretches out numberless tentacles of questioning and theory to grasp the meaning of the world; it asks inescapably about evil, and origins, and evolution, and destiny, and soul, and God. Religious "conversion" may come now, or religious doubt; religion may strengthen itself by self-attachment to the new impulses of love; or it may fight against the widening stream of desire in the soul, and awaken a hostility that for a while may rant in revengeful atheism.

It is about this time that youth discovers philosophy, and turns it into logic-bouts. The full heart flowers into song and dance; the esthetic sense is nourished with the overflow of desire; music and art are born. Discovering the world, youth discovers evil, and is horrified to learn the nature of his species. The principle of the family was mutual aid; but the principle of society is competition, the struggle for existence, the elimination of the weak and the survival of the strong. Youth, shocked, rebels, and calls upon the world to make itself a family, and give to youth the welcome and protection and comradeship of the home: the age of socialism comes. And then slowly youth is drawn into the gamble of this individualistic life; the zest of the game creeps into the blood; acquisitiveness is aroused and stretches out both hands for gold and power. The rebellion ends; the game goes on.

Finally, youth discovers love. It has known "puppy love," that ethereal prelude to the coming symphonies of flesh and soul; and it has known the lonely struggles of premature and uninformed desire. But these were only preliminaries that would deepen the spirit and make it ready for the self-abandonment of adoration.

See them in love, this boy and this girl; is there any evil this side of mortality that can balance the splendor of this good? The girl suddenly made quiet and thoughtful as the stream of life rises to conscious creation in her; the youth eager and restless, and yet all courtesy and gentleness, knowing the luxuries of courtship, aflame with something based in the hunger of the blood and yet something that rises to a marvelous tenderness and loyalty. Here is a fulfillment of long centuries of civilization and culture; here, in romantic love, more than in the triumphs of thought or the victories of power, is the topmost reach of human beings.

When we were young we married because romance had caught us up into devotion, but now our precarious and complex life delays marriage ever more and more beyond the age of love. What is youth to do in the increasing years between the coming of desire and the conquest of some place in the economic world that will warrant marriage? Let him answer who dares. And yet is it not time that we should be brave enough to face the issue, and understand that civilization must either restore early marriage or abandon love?

He who denounces the "immorality" of youth, and then stands by idle while financial caution postpones marriage, and therefore promotes promiscuity, and makes unnatural demands upon the sex to which love is life—such a man is a hypocrite or a fool. Desire is too strong to be dammed so unreasonably with moral prohibitions; its power has grown with every generation, for every generation is the result of its selected vigor; soon the flood of life will break through our insincerities and make new ways and morals for us while we shut our eyes.

Perhaps when it is too late we shall discover that we have sold the most precious thing in our civilization—the loyal love of a man for a woman—for the sake of the desolate security that cowards find in gold. Youth, if it were wise, would cherish love beyond all things else, keeping body and soul clean for its coming, lengthening its days with months of betrothal, sanctioning it with a marriage of solemn ritual, making all things subordinate to it resolutely. Wisdom, if it were young, would cherish love, nursing it with devotion, deepening it with sacrifice, vitalizing it with parentage, making all things subordinate to it till the end. Even though it consumes us in its service and overwhelms us with tragedy, even though it breaks us down with separations, let it be first. How can it matter what price we pay for love?

CHAPTER THREE

ON MIDDLE AGE

A nd so youth marries, and youth ends. A married man is already five years older the next day, and a married woman, too. Biologically, middle age begins with marriage; for then work and responsibility replace carefree play, passion surrenders to the limitations of social order, and poetry yields to prose. It is a change that varies with customs and climates: marriage comes late now in our modern cities, and adolescence lengthens; but among the peoples of the South and East marriage comes at the height of youth, and age on the heels of parentage.

"Young Orientals who exercise marital functions at thirteen," said G. Stanley Hall, "are worn out at thirty, and have recourse to aphrodisiacs. . . . Women in hot climates are often old at thirty. In the main it is probable that those who mature late age late." Perhaps if we could delay our sexual maturity till our economic maturity has come we would, by lengthening adolescence and education, rise to a higher plane of civilization than the past has ever known.

Each age of life has its virtues and its defects, its tasks and its delights. As Aristotle found excellence and wisdom in the golden mean, so the qualities of youth, maturity, and old age may be arranged to give a fair face to the central division of human life. For example:

YOUTH	MIDDLE AGE	OLD AGE
Instinct	Induction	Deduction
Innovation	Habit	Custom
Invention	Execution	Obstruction
Play	Work	Rest
Art	Science	Religion
Imagination	Intellect	Memory
Theory	Knowledge	Wisdom
Optimism	Meliorism	Pessimism
Radicalism	Liberalism	Conservatism
Absorption-in-future	Absorption-in-present	Absorption-in-past
Courage	Prudence	Timidity
Freedom	Discipline	Authority
Vacillation	Stability	Stagnation

Such a list could be continued indefinitely, piling truisms like Pelion on Ossa. Out of it at least this consolation emerges for middle age: that it is the epoch of achievement and establishment. For the exhilaration and enthusiasm of youth, life gives then the calm and pride of security and power, the sense of things not merely hoped for but accomplished.

At thirty-five a man is at the height of his curve, retaining enough of the passion of younger years, and tempering it with the perspective of widened experience and a more mature understanding. Perhaps there is some synchronism here with the cycle of sex, which reaches its zenith at about thirty-two, midway between puberty and menopause.

As we find a place in the economic world the rebellion of youth subsides; we disapprove of earthquakes when our feet are on the earth. We forget our radicalism then in a gentle liberalism—which is radicalism softened with the consciousness of a bank account. After forty we prefer that the world should stand still, that the moving picture of life should freeze into a tableau. Partly the increased conservatism of middle age is the result of wisdom, which perceives the complexity of institutions and the imperfections of desire; but partly it is the result of lowered energy, and corresponds to the immaculate morality of exhausted men. We perceive, at first incredulously and then with despair, that the reservoir of strength no longer fills itself after we draw upon it.

The discovery darkens life for some years; we begin to mourn the brevity of the human span, and the impossibility of wisdom or fulfillment within so limited a circle; we stand at the top of the hill, and without straining our eyes we can see, at its bottom, death. We work all the harder to forget that it is waiting for us; we turn our eyes back in memory to the days that were not darkened with its presence; we revel in the company of the young because they cast over us, transiently and incompletely, their divine carelessness of mortality. Hence it is in work and parentage that middle age finds its fulfillment and its happiness.

The commuter is the picture of middle age. He breakfasts between headlines, and kisses his wife and children a hurried good-bye; he rushes to the station, exchanges meteorological platitudes with his duplicates along the platform, reads his paper, walks precariously through Lower Manhattan's fruit and filth, and clings like a drowning man to a subterranean strap while he is whirled with seismic discomfort to his toil. Arrived, his importance subsides; instead of great decisions to be made he finds, for the most part, a soporific routine of repetitious details. He plods through them loyally, looks longingly at the clock that keeps him from his home, and thinks how pleasant it will be to spend the evening with his family. At five he rides again in suspended animation to his train, exchanges alcoholic audacities with his duplicates, and assumes a philosophic dignity as he contemplates the daily tragedies of the national game. At six he is home, and at eight he wonders why he hurried so.

For by this time he has explored the depths of love, and has found the war that lurks in its gentle guise. Familiarity and fatigue have cooled the fever in his flesh. His wife does not dress for him, only when he has gone away and is no longer in her mind; he sees her in a disheveled negligee, while all through the day he meets women powdered and primped and curled, whose charming knees and inviting frocks and encouraging smiles and aphrodisiac perfumes leave him hovering hourly over the abysses of disloyalty. But he tries hard to love his wife, and kisses her regularly and promptly twice a day. He has an escapade or two, discovers the dullness in adultery, thanks God that he has not been detected, and reconciles himself to prose. For the rest he mows his lawn, plays cards and golf, and dabbles amateurishly in local politics. The last recreation soon sours on him. In the end he concludes that the wisest words of tongue or pen were uttered by Candide: *"We must cultivate our garden."* He plants potatoes, and achieves a moderate peace.

In the interim his wife has learned something of life, too. In the romantic years she had been a goddess; suddenly she finds that she is a cook. The discovery is discouraging. Why should she maintain the laborious allurements of dress and rouge for a man who looks upon her as an economical substitute for a maid? Or she does not cook, and does not clean; these things, and many more, are done for her, and she is left free, respectable, and functionless all the livelong day. She spends her mornings making her toilette, and her afternoons reforming the proletariat; she reads about hygiene and maternity, and tells poor mothers how to bring up babies, when the harassed women merely wish to learn how to stop their coming. She attends extension classes, organizes clubs, and listens with romantic patience to peripatetic novelists and philosophers.

And then suddenly, somehow, she is a mother. She is pleased and terrified. Perhaps it will kill her to bear a child; not for a long time has she had the chance to do the wholesome work that would have fitted her physically for this fulfillment. But she is proud, too, and feels a new maturity; she is a woman now, and not an idle girl, not a domestic ornament or a sexual convenience anymore. She goes through her ordeal bravely; when she sees her child she weeps for a moment and then marvels at the child's unprecedented beauty. Fondly she slaves for it, through busy days and fragmentary nights, never having time to look for "happiness," and yet showing in her eyes a new radiance and delight. And now what is this new tenderness in the father's eyes, this new gentleness in the touch of his hands, this unwonted sincerity in his embrace, this new willingness to labor and cherish and protect? Perhaps here in the child, where one never thought to seek it, is the center of life, and the secret of content?

CHAPTER FOUR

ON OLD AGE

Men ought to die at their zenith, but they do not; and therefore youth and death meet each other as they walk the streets. At Columbia University, many years ago, a happy student, wandering among the bookshelves of the library, came abruptly face-to-face, round a turn in the stacks, with a bent and white-haired man of perhaps some eighty years. They looked at each other silently; but in his heart the young man said, "There, but for the lack of time, go I," and in his eyes the old man said, "I, too, was once young like you; hungry for knowledge, hopeful of achievement, eager for change. Now I spend my nights sleeplessly in remembering little things, and my days in poring over yellow newspapers that tell excitedly of the time when I was young." And once the youth paused in the street at the sight of an old man buttressed with sideboards and leaning on a cane, looking awed and timid at the Niagara of automobiles pouring down Fifth Avenue. The lined and sallow face, kindly but puzzled to irritation, showed the subtle tragedy of a generation left rudely behind by a tumultuously changing world. Perhaps it is for such souls that the mills of the gods grind exceedingly slow, lest the mind of man should break under the strain of endless transformations.

What is old age? Fundamentally, no doubt, it is a condition of the flesh, of protoplasm that finds inevitably the limit of its life. It is a physiological and psychological involution. It is a hardening of the arteries and categories, an arresting of thought and blood; a man is as old as his arteries, and as young as his ideas. The ability to learn decreases with each decade of our lives, as if the association fibers of the brain were accumulated and overlaid in inflexible patterns. New material seems no longer to find room, and recent impressions fade as rapidly as a politician's promises, or the public's memory of them. As decay proceeds, threads and unities are lost, and coordination wavers; the old man falls into a digressive circumstantiality, and De Quincey's "anecdotage" comes.

Then, just as the child grew more rapidly the younger it was, so the old man ages more quickly with every day. And just as the child was protected by insensitivity on its entry into the world, so old age is eased by an apathy of sense and will, and nature slowly administers a general anesthesia before she permits Time's scythe to complete the most major of operations.

As sensations diminish in intensity, the sense of vitality fades; the desire for life gives way to indifference and patient waiting; the fear of death is strangely mingled with the longing for repose. Perhaps then, if one has lived well, if one has known the full term of love and all the juice and ripeness of experience, one can die with some measure of content, clearing the stage for a better play.

But what if the play is never better, always revolving about suffering and death, telling endlessly the same idiotic tale?

There's the rub, and there's the doubt that gnaws at the heart of wisdom, and poisons age. Here is shameless adultery and brutal, calculating murder. Well, they have always been, and apparently they always will be. Here is a flood, sweeping before it a thousand lives and the labor of generations. Here are bereavements and broken hearts, and always the bitter brevity of love. Here still are the insolence of office and the law's delay, corruption in the judgment seat, and incompetence on the throne. Here is slavery, stupefying toil that makes great muscles and little souls.

Here and everywhere is the struggle for existence, life inextricably enmeshed with war. All life living at the expense of life, every organism eating other organisms forever. Here is history, a futile circle of infinite repetition: these youths with eager eyes will make the same errors as we, they will be misled by the same dreams; they will suffer, and wonder, and surrender, and grow old.

CHAPTER FIVE

ON DEATH

O nly one thing is certain in history, and that is decadence; only one thing is certain in life, and that is death. This can be the great tragedy of old age, that, looking back with inverted romantic eye, it may see only the suffering of mankind. It is hard to praise life when life abandons us, and if we speak well of it even then it is because we hope we shall find it again, of fairer form, in some realm of disembodied and deathless souls.

And yet what if it is for life's sake that we must die? In truth we are not individuals; and it is because we think ourselves such that death seems unforgivable. We are temporary organs of the race, cells in the body of life; we die and drop away that life may remain young and strong. If we were to live forever, growth would be stifled and youth would find no room on the earth. Death, like style, is the removal of rubbish, the circumcision of the superfluous.

We separate a portion of ourselves from the body that is aging, and call it a child; through our undiscourageable love we pass our vitality on to this new form of us before the old form dies; through parentage we bridge the chasm of the generations, and elude the enmity of death. Here, even in the flood, children are born; in the chaos of a car crowded with refugees, twins suddenly appear; there, solitary in a tree, and surrounded by raging waters, a mother nurses her babe. In the midst of death life renews itself immortally.

So wisdom may come as the gift of age, and seeing things in place, and every part in its relation to the whole, may catch that full perspective in which understanding pardons all. If it is one test of philosophy to give life a meaning that shall conquer death, wisdom will show that corruption comes only to the part, that life itself is deathless while we die.

Three thousand years ago a man thought that man might fly, and so he built himself wings, and Icarus—his son—trusting them and trying to fly, fell into the sea. Undaunted, life carried on the dream. Thirty generations passed, and Leonardo da Vinci, spirit made flesh, scratched across his drawings (drawings so beautiful that one catches one's breath with pain on seeing them) plans and calculations for a flying machine, and left in his notes a little phrase that, once heard, rings like a bell in the memory—"There shall be wings." Leonardo failed and died, but life carried on the dream. Generations passed, and men said man would never fly, for it was not the will of God. And then man flew, and the agelong challenge of the bird was answered. Life is that which can hold a purpose for three thousand years and never yield. The individual fails, but life succeeds. The individual is foolish, but life holds in its blood and seed the wisdom of generations. The individual dies, but life, tireless and undiscourageable, goes on, wondering, longing, planning, trying, mounting, longing.

Here is an old man on the bed of death, harassed by helpless friends and wailing relatives. What a terrible sight it is—this thin frame with loosened and cracking flesh, this toothless mouth in a bloodless face, this tongue that cannot speak and these eyes that cannot see! To this pass youth has come, after all its hopes and trials, to this pass middle age, after all its torment and its toil. To this pass health and strength and joyous rivalry (this arm once struck blows and fought for victory in virile games). To this pass knowledge, science, and wisdom. For seventy years this man with pain and effort gathered knowledge; his brain became the storehouse of a varied experience, the center of a thousand subtleties of thought and deed; his heart through suffering learned gentleness as his mind learned understanding; seventy years he grew from an animal into a man capable of seeking truth and creating beauty. But death is upon him, poisoning him, choking him, congealing his blood, gripping his heart, bursting his brain, rattling in his throat. Death wins.

Outside on the green boughs birds twitter gaily, and Chantecler sings his hymn to the sun. Light streams across the fields; buds open, and stalks confidently lift their heads; the sap mounts in the trees. Here are children; what is it that makes them so joyous, running madly over the dew-wet grass, laughing, calling, pursuing, eluding, panting for breath, inexhaustible? What energy, what spirit and happiness! What do they care about death? They will learn and grow and love and struggle and create, and lift life up one little notch, perhaps, before they die. And when they pass they will cheat death with their children, with parental care that will make their children a little finer than themselves.

Life wins.

CHAPTER SIX

OUR SOULS

These steeples, everywhere pointing upward, ignoring despair and lifting hope, these lofty city spires, or simple chapels in the hills—they rise at every step from the earth to the sky; in every village of every nation on the globe they challenge doubt and invite weary hearts to consolation. Is it all a vain delusion? Is there nothing beyond life but death, and nothing beyond death but decay? We cannot know. But as long as men suffer, those steeples will remain.

Now would seem an appropriate time to examine whether or not anything of us survives the apparent finality of our existence. This requires some definitions of things such as matter, space, time, sensation, perception, mind, self, consciousness, and soul. Kant took eight hundred pages to do this; but as my mind is not as complex as his, I shall be content with far less.

By *matter* I mean that which occupies space. Theoretical physics, which is becoming another metaphysics, reduces matter to an almost spaceless energy, but this strikes me as a form of mysticism. I continue to perceive objects that occupy space, and I believe that objects can exist whether I perceive them or not. I find this view confirmed by a million experiments and a billion fellow men, which is enough. I admit that the object is not known to me as it is independently of my perception; it is changed, as it enters my ken, by the structure and condition of my senses, by the nature of the intervening medium, and by the character and incidence of the light falling upon the object and upon my eyes. But if I do suppose that my perceptions created the object I can easily disillusion myself in Samuel Johnson's brusque way—by kicking a sturdy stone.

Space, subjectively, is the coexistence of perceptions—perceiving two objects at once, one to the right or left of, under or above, the other; objectively, it is the possibility and medium of motion. Time, subjectively, is the conscious sequence of perceptions—one after the other; objectively, it is the possibility of change. The trees will grow and wither whether I perceive them or not; seasons will succeed one another whether or not there is an eye to watch their procession; dying trees may fall even if no ear is near to hear their crash. The world is not "my idea," as Schopenhauer called it; it is a stern reality of which you and I are passing spawns.

If I define matter as that which occupies space, I must conclude that mind is immaterial, since, to my direct and repeated introspection, it gives no sign of occupying space. It embraces a mile with no more effort than in contemplating an inch. By *mind* I mean the totality of perceptions, memories, and ideas in an organism, sometimes with consciousness thereof. A sensation is the feeling of an external stimulus or an internal condition. It may be unconscious and produce an unconscious reaction, as when you tickle the sole of my foot while I sleep and my toes curl up in a reflex action. A sensation becomes a perception when awareness ascribes it to a cause or place—"a pain in the ear," "a thunderclap."

Sensations, perceptions, memories, and ideas have material correlates in the nervous system, but they are something added to these correlates; it is this something that we can become aware of in introspection. I know that David Hume amused himself by reducing mind to a stream of perceptions or ideas, but he did not take himself very seriously. In addition to that succession of mental states there is, by the direct witness of introspection, a sense of continuity and personality constituting the "self"; there is, or can be, a consciousness which distinguishes waking from sleeping, and perception from memory. This has been a thorn in the metaphysics of every materialist.

At this point the psychoanalyst reminds me that much of my personality and my thinking is influenced, at times directed, by the "subconscious mind." I would rather call this the physiological self—the storing, in our nervous system, of past (even prenatal, even racial) sensations, actions, desires, and fears. These can enter into our dreams, when there is no waking conscious self to check past memory with present perception; and they can enter into our waking consciousness when some present experience arouses a related memory stored in the nerves. Such dormant recollections are part of the self and the soul; consciousness is not all of the soul, but only the soul's supreme achievement.

By *the soul*, as distinct from the mind, I mean an inner directive and energizing force in every body, and in every cell and organ of a body. It is closely associated with the breath (which, like the soul, was once termed *spiritus*), and it gradually dies if breathing permanently stops; but it is more than respiration, for it can rise from mere breathing to the subtlest functions of the body or the mind. When I introspect I perceive not merely sensations and ideas but desire, will, ambition, and pride as vital phases of *me*. Spinoza was right: *"desiderium ipsa essentia hominis"*—desire is the very essence of man. We are living flames of desire until we admit final defeat. Will is desire expressed in ideas that become actions unless impeded by contrary or substitute desires and ideas. Character is the sum of our desires, fears, propensities, habits, abilities, and ideas.

It is this soul or *psyche*, this steaming fountain of desires and thoughts, that forms the body and the face, limited by heredity and environment, and following the lines upon which ancestral souls have molded ancestral forms. When the amoeba extends itself into a temporary arm to clutch and enclose some wanted object, desire is molding that arm; and if such desires are so expressed through many lives and generations, the soul or directive force of the embryo may generate a permanent arm. I leave Darwin here, and revert with cautious modifications to Lamarck. I believe that in everything there is some formative force like that which I call soul. So I echo Spinoza again: *"omnia quodammodo animata"*—all things are in some way animated—even if it is only the dance of electrons in an apparently lifeless stone.

With diffidence and humility I depart from Spinoza in rejecting determinism. For determinism would make consciousness a superfluous encumbrance, and I doubt if so remarkable a development would have persisted if it had no value for survival. Part of its value is that it can serve as a rehearsal stage for testing diverse possible responses to a situation, imagining or forecasting the results of each potential response in the light of remembered experience, and letting the rehearsal affect the final action. Delayed reaction allows time for every important aspect of a situation to enter consciousness and to arouse a reply; in this way, response can be intelligent and adequate. If consciousness had no effect upon action, if every response was a mechanical reaction to a mechanical stimulus, waking life would be but another dream; unconscious forces would determine every perception, feeling, and idea.

I admit that in bare logic determinism seems irrefutable. Each moment in the history of the universe seems to follow inevitably from the condition and components of the preceding moment, and this from its predecessor, until every line of Shakespeare's plays finds its distant cause and explanation in some gaseous primeval nebula. This is harder to believe than any medieval miracle story. I incline to trust my immediate internal perception beyond any parade of syllogisms. How many things have been "proved" by "logic" and then discarded by later logicians—Euclidian propositions by Gauss and Riemann, Newtonian physics by Einstein. Logic itself is a human creation, and may be ignored by the universe.

There is an escape from the mechanical argument if we believe, as I do, that all nature includes some power of spontaneity, which becomes more and more complex as we rise from gases to human beings. In humans, besides heredity, environment, and circumstance (the determinist trinity), there is the expansive, driving, "procreant urge" of the soul; growth would be unintelligible without it. In addition to mechanical forces operating in me there is *me*, no mere machinery of sensation, memory, and response, but a force and will bearing the imprint and character of my self. I do not know what modest measure of freedom and origination I enjoy, but when I introspect I see no mechanism, but ambition, desire, will. Desire, not experience, is the essence of life; experience becomes the tool of desire in the enlightenment of mind and the pursuit of ends.

But if there is any element of freedom in my actions how can these find an opening, a way of operating, in an external world allegedly subject to the laws of mechanics and a deterministic fatality? They can because that external world may itself be no blind machine but a scene of diverse, often conflicting, vitalities and wills; and the "laws" of mechanics may be only the approximate average result, in the large, of those abounding forces. Physics itself seems to be moving toward such a conclusion, as in Werner Heisenberg's "principle of indeterminacy," and in Niels Bohr's conception of a duplex world—one internal and "concave," the other external and "convex," each with its own ways and laws.[1] Or as Spinoza put it, reality is one substance with everywhere two (among many) attributes or aspects—material extension and spaceless thought. We are among those parts of reality that can perceive—now in the body, now in the mind—both the external form and the internal life.[2]

Though I am fond of my unique soul, I do not expect it to survive the complete death of my body. Death is the breakup of the human soul—i.e., of the life-giving, form-molding force—of an organism into those partial souls that animate individual parts of the body; so these lesser souls can for a time continue the growth of hair and nails on a corpse. And when the corpse completely disintegrates there will be souls, or inner energizing powers, even in the "inorganic" fragments that remain. But my soul as me is bound up with my organized and centrally directed body, and with my individual memories, desires, and character; it must suffer disintegration as my body decays.

Here again I depart from my favorite philosopher, Spinoza. You will recall that toward the end of his *Ethics* he dallied with the idea of a kind of intellectual immortality: we can feel ourselves immortal, he suggested, insofar as we view things or ideas *sub specie aeternitatis*—in the perspective of eternity; then our thoughts will be immortal in the sense that they will be immune to time; we shall to that degree be part of the divine mind, which sees all things in an eternal light. Santayana comforted his materialism with a similar fantasy.[3] But which of us has ever seen, or can ever see, things in the perspective of eternity, or be ever sure that he knows the truth?

I am quite content with mortality; I should be appalled at the thought of living forever, in whatever paradise. As I move on into my nineties my ambitions moderate, my zest in life wanes; soon I shall echo Caesar's *Jam satis vixi*—"I have already lived enough." When death comes in due time, after a life fully lived, it is forgivable and good. If in my last gasps I say anything contrary to this bravado, pay no attention to me. We must make room for our children.

CHAPTER SEVEN

OUR GODS

Y you will not need to be told, now, that I am a theological
cal skeptic, believing in neither the warlike God of the
Hebrews nor the punishing and rewarding God of the
Christians. I see many evidences of order in the universe, but
also many conditions that seem to me disorderly, as in the reckless whimsies of meteors, or the arrogant deviations of plane-
tary orbits from the paths that our geometry would have
required; however, my conceptions of order and disorder, as of
beauty and sublimity and ugliness, are subjective; they are, so
to speak, my prejudices, since my mind can deal better with
things when I have put order into them and the universe has no
obligations to follow my preferences.

I see many evidences of design in nature and myself, many
indications of a cosmic spirit experimenting to find adjustments of means and organs to ends and desires; but I also see
many instances of organs imperfectly adapted to functions
and purposes (like the eye as Helmholtz criticized it), and of
events that suggest, from a human point of view, a cruel in-

stead of a kindly cosmic power, as in that Lisbon earthquake (1755) which slaughtered thousands of pious souls worshiping their God in church. "Nature" obviously cared no more for Spinoza than for the tubercle bacillus that killed him at the age of forty-four.

There is so much suffering in the world, and so much of it apparently undeserved, so much war, destruction, crime, corruption, and savagery, even in religious organizations like the medieval Church, that one finds it hard to believe that all this exists by permission of an all-powerful and benevolent deity. And yet there have been millions of Christians who interpreted these evils as deliberately willed by their God. How barbarous seems to us now the Calvinist doctrine of a Supreme Being who selects, among his human creatures before they have been conceived, those whom he will receive into heaven for everlasting happiness and those whom he will condemn to a hell of endless torture, regardless of whether they have lived lives of virtue or of vice.

It was the God of Christian theology whose death was so joyfully proclaimed in Nietzsche's *Also sprach Zarathustra* (1883); it is that God whom some young Christian theologians have in mind when they agree that "God is dead." Periodically, in history, man's conception of God changes as man's knowledge and moral sense improve; and these epochal transvaluations can upset not only philosophers and saints but also whole nations and eras. We live in such an age, when the revelations of science, and history, and the ethics of Christ, have made it impossible for developed minds to believe in that "grim beard of a God" who frightened our forbearers into decency. In this sense it was Christ who killed Jehovah.

The history of humanity might be written in terms of the

avatars of God—the repeated death of an old god to make room for a deity fitted to the rising knowledge and moral level of a race. A list of the diverse gods that men at one time or another have worshipped would make quite a directory of the changing skies. The supreme deities ran into hundreds, the minor deities into thousands. If past generations could return to earth they would be scandalized to learn that most of the gods they prayed to are today known only to anthropologists. Every people has in every epoch reinterpreted God after its own fashion, and has been willing to die, or at least to kill, in defense of that passing conception. So the historian is prepared to see the idea of God change again.

From the moment when Copernicus announced that the Earth, which had been the footstool of God, was but a minimal fraction of the universe, the old tribal deity began to die, and men heard a voice commanding them to enlarge their idea of God to suit the universe that astronomy was opening to human view.

Darwin furthered the transformation. As the astronomer had lost the Earth in space, the biologist lost man in the infinity of time, in the long procession of transitory species that had walked the earth or swum the sea or flown the air; man became a mere line in Nature's interminable odyssey. But it was Darwin, too, who opened a way to what John Morley called "the next great task of science—to create a new religion for humanity." Evolution, far from supporting the mechanistic philosophy of Herbert Spencer, revealed the essence of the cosmic process as not "matter" but life. And how could a machine evolve? We are compelled to think of evolution as active, not passive, not as the forming of organisms by environment and chance, but as the painstaking modification of environments and the partial regulation of chance by organisms endowed with the ability to experiment and to learn, not as a fortuitous concourse of aimless variations, but as the insatiable desire that creates organ after organ, molds the body in the image of the will, and remakes the face of the earth. Life itself can be the new God.

It will sound like childish sentiment and poor poetry, but I report it as a matter of fact repeatedly observed, that I have often felt, in the presence of growing things, an emotion that reminds me of the childhood piety with which I approached the Communion railing, or mumbled my way through the Stations of the Cross. I cannot look at any green shoot sprouting from the soil without feeling that in that mystic presence I am closer to the essence of reality than when my grandson tries in vain to explain to me the marvels of the atom.

This tree—I see it pushing its roots ever more deeply and widely into the soil, yet lifting itself up to the sky as if in prayer for light and warmth, spreading its branches and unfolding a hundred thousand leaves to breathe the air and catch the sun; I feel in myself the same lust for light and growth; this tree and I are kindred souls sharing the same hunger and the same life. I see fond parents frolicking with their children in the park, and I think that they, too, are part of life's litany. The poorest Madonna, sitting on the steps of her tenement and nursing her child, seems to me a form and symbol of that living force which hides behind all mechanisms and moves, as Dante said, "the sun and the other stars."

This, then, is the God I worship: the persistent and creative Life that struggles up from the energy of the atom to make the earth green with growth, to stir the youth with ambition and the girl with tender longing, to mold the form of woman, to agitate geniuses, to guide the art of Phidias, and to justify itself in Spinoza and Christ. I know that there are other aspects of reality than this life; that Nature is rich in terrors as well as in beauty and development; all the more should I reverence and help all growing things. This is a very old philosophy; otherwise I would distrust it.

Is my God personal? No—and why should it be? Personality belongs only to the parts of creation, not to the creative force; personality is separateness, a special form of will and character. The God I worship could not be such a separate and partial self; it is the sum and source of that universal vitality of which our little egos are abstracted fragments and experimental proliferations.

I am prepared to have you put me down as an atheist, since I have reluctantly abandoned belief in a personal and loving God. But I am loath to leave the word *God* out of my life and creed. I will respect your definition of deity, I will honor that of the lovable girls who attend a Catholic college just below the hill on which I have a home; and perhaps (since we are all drops of water trying to analyze the sea) you will allow me to have my definition, too. I have rejected materialism, I have accepted mind as the reality most directly known to me, and I have pictured the world as a scene not of blind mechanism but of striving and creative life. Let me then keep the term *God* for the inventive vitality and abounding fertility of Nature, the eon-long struggle of "matter" to rise from atomic energy to intelligence, consciousness, and informed and deliberate will, to statesmen, poets, saints, artists, musicians, scientists, and philosophers. Let me have something to worship!

I consider myself a Christian in the literal and difficult sense of sincerely admiring the personality and ethics of Christ, and making a persistent effort to behave like a Christian. I am not quite a saint. I have on several occasions attended and furtively enjoyed theatrical displays featuring the female form. Even in my nineties, I have felt a strong erotic urge, which my recent illness seemed to have knocked out of me; but already I feel it coming back. I suspect that I am a pagan as well as a Christian, respecting the pleasures of the senses as well as those of the mind, even while wishing that I could be as complete a Christian as Christ. But I have tried. Ariel and I have received substantial royalties from our books, but we yield more than half of our income to taxes, and we give away half of the rest. We have always lived and dressed very simply, and if we have traveled much it was almost always for toilsome research; I hate travel and love my home. I have never, so far as I can remember, returned evil for evil; have never hated or condemned anyone; have never supported a war except that of America against Japan and Germany in 1941.

If I could live another life, endowed with my present mind and mood, I would not write history or philosophy, but would devote myself to establishing an association of men and women free to have any tolerant theology or no theology at all, but pledged to follow as far as possible the ethics of Christ, including chastity before marriage, fidelity within it, extensive charity, and peaceful opposition to any but the most clearly defensive war. I can imagine what fun the wits of the world could have with this paragraph, and I know how unpopular and precarious my proposed fellowship of semi-saints would be; but I would rather contribute a microscopic mite to improving the conduct of men and statesmen than write the one hundred best books.

CHAPTER EIGHT

ON RELIGION

Some religions, like early Buddhism, were without belief in God; indeed, on March 31, 1967, news came that the Buddhists of South Vietnam objected to admitting the idea of God into their new constitution. I am not qualified to speak about the Asiatic religions, but I have some intimate acquaintance with Christianity.

Ariel is probably right in smiling at me as still a Catholic below the neck. I received in childhood and youth a pious training by nuns and priests, and I have only the fondest memories of them. I recall with some nostalgia the modest girls in the parochial schools which I attended in Massachusetts and New Jersey, and the lovely litanies of the Virgin, and the pleasant hymns that we youngsters of both sexes (there were only two sexes then) sang under the leadership of our devoted and respected teachers. I remember with gratitude my seven years under Jesuit educators in "academy" and college, though it was in my sophomore year (1905) with them that my independent reading of Darwin and Spencer melted my inherited theology.

Only the best side of Christianity was presented to us—a loving God, a gentle Christ, an ethics of kindness and chastity and filial devotion; very little was said about Satan or hell, and probably those dedicated nuns had never heard of the Inquisition. I was their pet, for I was bright, alert, and troublesome, and perhaps they knew that my parents had destined me for the priesthood. They took me into the arcane of their simple nunnery, and fed me the most convincing pies.

Of all the priests whom I have known the finest was Father (later Monsignor) James Mooney, stern but kind, ascetic and devout, burning himself out in guiding youths in Seton Hall College and Seminary. I entered the seminary in 1909, partly to please him, partly to avoid a crisis in my family, and partly in the hope of turning the Catholic Church in America toward cooperation with the socialist movement. For by 1906 I had replaced my Christian creed with a dream of socialism as the hope of the world; so Utopia comes up as heaven goes down. By 1911 I found it impossible to continue my pretenses to orthodoxy; I left the seminary, causing much grief to my parents, and years of mental chaos and loneliness to myself.

Those who were deeply indoctrinated with Catholicism in their adolescence never quite recover from the collapse of their faith, for Catholicism is the most attractive of religions, rich in drama, poetry, and art, and tender to the flesh. Doubtless we denuded ones now idealize that faith, forgetting in it the elements of absurdity, terror, and intolerance, and remembering the creed and the ritual as making us participants in a magnificent epos that gave meaning and dignity to the simplest life, disciplined us into decency, and brought consolation to millions of souls suffering pain, bereavement, or defeat. To me the "death of God" and the slow decay of Christianity in the edu-

cated classes of Christendom constitute the profoundest tragedy in modern Western history, of far deeper moment than the
great wars or the competition between capitalism and communism. I felt this when, in 1931, I wrote *On the Meaning of Life*,
and asked prominent persons in Europe and America what life
meant for them now that God had disappeared. I went
through, in those years from 1906 to 1931, all the wondering
and anguish and sense of irreparable loss that afflicted the existentialists of France in the years that followed.

I have tried to keep some hold on the religion of my youth
by interpreting its basic doctrines as symbols that gave popular
expression to philosophic truths. I can rephrase "original sin" as
man's inherited disposition to follow those instincts of pugnacity, sexual promiscuity, and greed which may have been necessary in the hunting stage of human history, but which need a
variety of controls in an organized society that guarantees its
members protection against violence, theft, and rape; we are
born with the taint of ancestral passions in our blood. In the
expulsion of "our first parents" from paradise because they had
eaten the fruit of the tree of knowledge I can see a forecast of
Ecclesiastes' somber warning—"He that increaseth knowledge
increaseth sorrow," for knowledge can destroy a happy inno-
cence and many a comforting or inspiring delusion. I can interpret Adam's "sin," like so many of our own, as man's forgivable
surrender to the witchery of woman and the ecstasy of her
charms.

Heaven and hell remain for me not places in another world,
but states of mind often associated with virtue and vice in this
life. I can think of Christ as the personification of godliness
because—barring his rejection of his mother (Matt. 13:54–58)
and some bitter words about hell (Matt. 13:37–42; Mark 9:48;

Luke 16:25)—he preached a code of conduct which, if generally practiced, would make even poverty an earthly paradise. I can praise Christianity for winning wider acceptance of moral ideas by transforming these into pictures, narratives, dramas, and art, and thereby helping to tame the unsocial impulses of mankind. In this sense I could think of Church leaders as religious statesmen who, whatever they themselves might believe, used the Bible, theology, and ritual as aids in transforming congenital savages into responsible and orderly citizens. I have at times dreamed of a reconciliation between religion and philosophy through a "gentlemen's agreement" in which educated men would leave uncriticized the pictorial and consolatory creeds of simple souls, and the Church (Catholic, Protestant, and Jewish) would refrain from hampering freedom of thought in circles and publications accessible only to persons with time and capacity for abstract thought. There have been persons and places in Christian history when such an entente in some measure operated: Italy under Leo X, England in the Victorian compromise, Vienna in the days of Schnitzler and Freud.

Only a similar compromise could reconcile me to the coming control of American life by the Catholic Church. That Church already controls South America, and it is powerful in Mexico and French Canada. In the United States its future ascendancy is guaranteed by the higher birthrate of its adherents. A Princeton University analysis issued in April 1967 reported that "Roman Catholic wives were having, and expected to have, 21 percent more children than non-Catholic wives."[1]

The differential between Catholic and non-Catholic fertility is diminishing through increasing use of birth control by Catholic women; but the generally higher birthrate of the less educated as compared with the better-educated classes, the prudent opposition of the Church to mechanical contraceptives, and the esprit de corps of the Catholic population and clergy forecast a continued rise, even if at a slower rate, of the Catholic proportion in our population. Many of our larger cities are already under Catholic control; that control will in the near future extend to many legislatures; by 2100 it may include Congress and the presidency. A like triumph of the birthrate over that of the Reformation and the Enlightenment is taking place in French Switzerland and Western Germany, overcoming Calvin and Luther, and may even prevail in France, laughing at Voltaire.

What kind of men will those triumphant priests be? Will they be as tolerant as Leo X and Benedict XIV, or as dogmatic and domineering as Gregory VII and Innocent III? Today the Catholic hierarchy is intolerant where it is supreme, as in Spain and South America; it favors and needs toleration where Catholic power is checked by other religions, or by secular education, or by the current prestige of science. But the prestige of science may be ruined by a war murderous beyond any precedent, and the independence of secular education in state universities and colleges will increasingly be subject to legislatures increasingly Catholic. We have seen federal help to education in the United States held up by Catholic influence until the president and Congress agreed to extend aid to Catholic schools and colleges, apparently overriding the constitutional separation of church and state. Freedom of ecclesiastical property from taxation also seems to violate the Constitution, since in effect it is governmental aid to religion; and the spread of such tax-exempt property places an ever-greater burden upon the tax-paying public. The tax-free wealth of the churches in America is growing at a rate where it may repeat in the next century the crisis of France in 1792—a government unable to meet its obligations despite the discouragingly high taxation of its people, while vast areas of ecclesiastical property enjoy tax-free status.

In any case I consider the "death of God" to have been as exaggerated as Mark Twain's. Since all men, even twins, are born unequal in some aspect of physical or mental capacity, an inequality of status and possessions seems unavoidable short of a dictatorship complete enough to abolish all liberty; and such dictatorships do not last. Standards of living may rise in interludes of peace, but the least affluent nations and classes (however better off than their similars in previous centuries) will still feel and protest against their exclusion from the possessions and privileges of the rich.

Historically such "underprivileged" nations and classes have sought consolation in supernatural beliefs, dignifying themselves by association with mystic powers, and tempering the sting of poverty with hopes of a better fortune in another world. Chronic illness, deformity, or grief may serve like poverty to generate such creeds, and social heredity can sustain these, even in nations economically prosperous. So many are the functions that supernatural religion fulfills that the skeptic must learn to make his peace with it, only hoping that the love which radiated from Christ will overcome the fearful intolerance of empowered creeds.

CHAPTER NINE

ON A DIFFERENT
SECOND ADVENT

In the year 1883 Friedrich Nietzsche, the most important European philosopher since Immanuel Kant, announced that "God is dead."[1] Five years later he predicted that the time would come when history would be divided between "Before and After Nietzsche."[2] He was confident that his attacks upon Christianity and democracy would be fatal to those creeds, and that the twentieth century would see their disappearance.

His prediction may still be verified. Half of Christendom has officially rejected Christianity, and in the other half the death of God is the chief topic of theologians. Half of Christendom has repudiated democracy as a window dressing for the rule of money over simplicity, and in the Latin part of the other half democracy is being gradually replaced by authoritarian rule. Nearly all of Europe and America has put aside the ethics of Christ as incompatible with military vigor and designs, and have adopted Nietzsche's "master morality" of "the will to power." Two world wars have seriously wounded Christianity; a third may end it as a force in history. Has the Age of Nietzsche begun?

Today the soul of Western man knows a double disillusionment, for in the space of one lifetime it has lost the bright faith of its childhood and the hopeful utopias of its youth. Where shall we find again a belief to give us stimulus, a conscience to give us decency, a new devotion to give nobility to our little span?

To prescribe for a religion is as presumptuous as to indict a whole nation—although the latter is no rare performance in this ideological age. Philosophers do not make or change religions; such epochal transformations require a profound longing in the hearts of millions, the moral passion of some saint, and the patient compromises of some organizing genius; so to a despondent Hellenistic world came the message of Christ, still within the Mosaic Law, until Paul broadened it to welcome all men. Religions are not made by the intellect, else they would never touch the soul or reach the masses, or achieve longevity. A successful religion without incredible elements would be incredible; the imagination must be stirred, some vision or poem must be superimposed by a creative faith upon an existence so dulled with drudgery and prose, so weighted with suffering and defeat. We cannot expect a religion to be a body of scientific propositions.

We may, however, ask that a religion shall soften the heart of man, that it shall inspire courage, conscience, and charity, that it shall make the strong a little more generous to the weak, that it shall mitigate the rigor of competition and the brutality of war. Since the only real progress is moral development, a religion faithful to these aims would (other things being equal) be the best faith and antidote for this factious and warring world.

In the moral doctrine of Christ Christianity offered precisely such a religion. If we examine our memories we shall find that what stirred us in our native faith was not a body of doctrine but the ethics and story of Christ, the challenge to behave as if all men were brothers, and the example of a life that lived up to this seemingly impossible ideal. It is difficult to imagine how anyone could improve upon this outline of a faith for the modern soul. Through all the adventures of the mind among philosophies and creeds the figure of Christ remains the most appealing in history. We do not need a new religion so much as a return to the old one in its essentials and its simplicity. All over the world it has been found easy to interest people in Christ, but hard to keep them for the theological division of Christianity. For all the world will hear gladly the story of a man who died that there might be good will among men and peace among states. What else is the world longing for today?

Let us "see visions and dream dreams." We picture one after another of the great Christian denominations meeting in enthusiastic assembly, redefining Christianity as *sincere acceptance of the moral ideals of Christ*, and inviting to their membership any person, of whatever race or creed, who is willing to receive those ideals as the test and goal of his conduct and development.

We picture such an invitation blazoned over the portals of thousands of churches—and of temples and mosques, at least in America. For Islam has long since accepted Christ as one of the supreme prophets, and Judaism could proudly reclaim Christ as its own (as he was), if he were not made an agent and symbol of hatred and inquisitions. We do not propose the abandonment of theology; we contemplate a congregation in which each member will be free to form or hold his own theology or philosophy, tolerantly extending a like freedom to his associates. If this seems impracticable, consider the success, the corporate spirit and ritual, of our fraternal or service societies, which include a generous variety of religious and political beliefs. Shall we practice this Christian brotherhood in our secular associations and exclude it from our churches?

We picture the rituals of the denominations retaining in like manner their independence and diversity, but, in their general gathering, stressing more and more with each year their common moral elements; allowing a poetical or symbolical interpretation of their theology to those who prefer it, restoring, it might well be, the weekly common meal as a unifying ceremony, and using and inspiring, as in medieval days, all the arts to give substance and color to their dream.

We picture a great union of creeds and sects preaching the ethics of Christ, a church vigorous with its new consolidated strength, ready to meet the competition of bizarre cults and nationalistic infatuations, a church gathering into one fellowship all the racial groups in America and Europe, offering a moral code that would help men to raise themselves out of the corruption and violence that threaten to consume our civilization. We believe that such a Christianity would draw to itself the Buddhas and Kabirs, the Lao-tzus and Kagawas, the Platos and Zenos, the Spinozas and Einsteins, the Jeffersons and Franklins, the Lincolns and Whitmans, the Tolstoys and Tagores of time to come. We see the intellectual classes returning to the temple, glad to mingle once more with the simplest worshippers, happy to feel a community of soul beneath a diversity of thought, to have again something that they believe and revere, to honor with all their hearts an ideal that, even if every generation opposes it, will never die.

Since we cannot expect human beings, in any large number, or in the near future, to make the Sermon on the Mount the actual rule of their lives, shall we not fall into an impracticable perfectionism if we define Christianity as the practice of the principles of Christ? Certainly; and therefore we define it rather as the sincere acceptance of those principles. Perhaps Christ meant the full code only for his preaching disciples, not for the laity. For the rest of us we can only promise to do our best, obstinately to *try* to treat all men as brothers; this is all that Christianity demands. To exact of all men a saintly level of selflessness would be to condemn Christianity to everlasting hypocrisy.

Even of those who preach the Good News of peace and good will we should not expect the literal practice of the master's counsels; he himself fell short of them when for a moment he spoke of hell. We believe that many saints would appear in such a moral faith, men like St. Francis or Spinoza or Ramakrishna; but we know ourselves too well to expect this of many men. At most we presume that our teachers and leaders would brook no restraint upon their inculcation of the Christian code, and that, if necessary, they would leave the costly pulpit and preach, like Christ, along the highways and byways of men. We trust, too, that a strengthened and purified Church would honor the freedom of mind in science and print and speech, and would recognize that the good and the beautiful may shine out in sages, rebels, and poets as well as in prophets and saints. Indeed the new Church would welcome the accumulation of a second Bible, recording the most inspiring thoughts and actions of every race of men. Who will be the Plutarch of the moral heroes of history?

We know how much our pride and prejudice, our fearful hate and unwilling ignorance, obstruct the fulfillment of this dream; we do not expect this second coming of Christ to take place before these mortal eyes. But already the fulfillment has in some measure begun. There are in America and Europe thousands of clergymen who are ready and eager for the Christianity of Christ. It is we, the laity, who hold them back, who insist upon our inherited orthodoxies, and who hesitate to sit in the same pew with one whose beliefs differ in any article from our own. Because of us Christianity is torn and weak at the very moment when it is challenged to stand up for its faith against the god of war.

We must give courage to our leaders to lead us, to re-create for us a Christianity that would be intelligible to Christ. Let us lift up to them, as modestly as the bold words will allow, the most Christian of all hymns, which the most inspired of all poets addressed to the most Christian of all men:

> *My spirit to yours dear brother . . .*
> *I specify you with joy, O my comrade, to salute you, and to*
>   *salute those who are with you, before and since, and*
>   *those to come also,*
> *That we all labor together transmitting the same charge and*
>   *succession,*
> *We few equals indifferent of lands, indifferent of times,*
> *We, enclosers of all continents, all castes, allowers of all*
>   *theologies,*
> *Compassionaters, perceivers, rapport of men,*
> *We walk silent among disputes and assertions, but reject not*
>   *the disputers nor any thing that is asserted,*
> *We hear the bawling and din, we are reach'd at by divisions,*

jealousies, recriminations on every side,
They close peremptorily upon us to surround us, my comrade,
Yet we walk unheld, free, the whole earth over, journeying up
and down till we make our ineffaceable mark upon time
and the diverse eras,
Till we saturate time and eras, that the men and women of
races, ages to come, may prove brethren and lovers as
we are.

CHAPTER TEN

ON RELIGION AND MORALS

S hall we define our terms? Historically, *religion* has been the worship of supernatural powers. Webster defines *morality* as "the quality of that which conforms to right ideals or principles of human conduct." But who is to determine which ideals are right? The individual himself? Reckless souls have tried to define the right as any conduct which their conscience approves of; but in that case Casanova and the Marquis de Sade were moral, for they tried to live up to their proclaimed ideal, which was to seduce or beat as many women as other commitments would allow.

The word *moral*, of course, is from the Latin *mos, moris*, meaning "custom"; we may agree that what at a given time or place is considered moral will depend upon the mores, customs, or standards prevailing in the group. Personally I should define *morality* as the consistency of private conduct with public interest as understood by the group. It implies a recognition by the individual that his life, liberty, and development depend upon social organization, and his willingness, in return, to adjust himself to the needs of the community.

On the basis of this definition the Church can make an impressive case for itself as an indispensable bulwark of morality. It claims that the current relaxation of morals in Western Europe and America is due principally to the decline of religious belief, and that the unforgivable criminals in the alleged debacle are the *philosophes* of the eighteenth century, and their thousands of intellectual progeny who have joined in the attack upon the Church. I can imagine some irate cardinal belaboring the infidels:

You ignorant fools! When will you grow up enough to understand that your individual security and survival are the gifts of social order; that social order can be maintained only through the influence of the family, the school, and the Church; that no number of laws or policemen can replace the moral discipline inculcated by parents, teachers, and priests; that in attacking these formative and protective institutions you are sapping the dykes that have been raised through the labor and wisdom of centuries against the individualistic, disorderly, and savage impulses that lurk in the hearts of men? What will you do when parental authority has been rejected by "liberated" youth, when young ruffians make life a daily torture for the teachers in your schools, when your religious leaders are derided and defamed, when the life-sustaining structure of Christian doctrine has been weakened, when your public officials smile at their own corruption, when organized crime is more powerful than your police and your courts, when your literature and your theaters madden men with incitements to sex, when your daughters are raped, or seduced and abandoned by sex-crazed men, when you dare not walk the streets at night for fear of robbery, assault, or assassination? There is only one thing you can do: come back penitently to religion, and beg the Church to put into your children the love of Christ and the fear of a living, avenging God.

I am touched by this argument, for I, too, have shot my pebbles against the Church, and now I am not at all confident that man's unsocial impulses can be controlled by a moral code shorn of religious belief. Have I been an "unforgivable criminal" and an "ignorant fool"? I might plead that I tried to be fair to the Catholic Church in *The Age of Faith* and *The Reformation.* I gave the attack upon Christianity 182 of 799 pages in *The Age of Voltaire,* for that attack was the most important— the most widely, deeply, lastingly influential—event of the eighteenth century; but I stated the case for the Church with considerable sympathy in the epilogue to that book. I could never quite make up my mind whether I was an anticlerical hero or a lover harboring a secret affection for a deserted ideal.

The ideal was deserted because it had disowned itself. The Church had overlaid the incomparable ethics of Jesus with a complex structure of incredible dogma echoing St. Paul and mostly unknown to Christ, and with an omnipresent incubus of organization and theocratical police lying heavy upon the human mind, ready to stifle any independent thought by using the powers of the state to imprison, confiscate, and kill. The local priests and nuns still remembered (and often practiced) Christianity, but the hierarchy forgot it in a lust for unassailable and infallible authority.

The Church had begun with the Prince of Peace, who had bidden Peter put his sword back into its sheath; it had become a warrior using swords, pikes, and guns against the Albigensians of

France and the Jews of Spain. The lowly carpenter of Nazareth had been replaced by a pope more richly housed than most emperors, and controlling more wealth than most states. In disputes between oppressors and oppressed the hierarchy had almost always supported the oppressors and suppressed the oppressed. The success of humanists and humanitarians in freeing the mind and the serf emboldened men to demand the taming of this dogmatic, obscurantist, intolerant, and reactionary power.

Has the weakening of that power been the main cause of our moral decline? No. It has been one factor among many, but not the chief. The principal and overspreading cause of our moral "decay" has been the Industrial Revolution. Almost every aspect of that economic convulsion has affected morality. As examples:

1. The passage from rural mutual surveillance to concealment of the individual in the urban multitude has almost ended the force of neighborly opinion to control personal behavior.

2. On the farm, till 1900, the family was the unit of economic production, and the authority of the father was strengthened by his economic leadership and by family solidarity. Under industrialism the corporation and the employee are the units of production; the family is dispersed to follow scattered jobs; the son becomes financially independent of the father; parental authority loses its economic base.

3. On the farm the youth reached economic maturity—i.e., the ability to support a wife and children—almost as soon as he reached biological maturity—i.e., the ability to have children; marriage came early, and premarital continence was less difficult than in our contemporary industrial soci-

ety, where the deferment of economic maturity has delayed marriage and made continence difficult.

4. On the farm the wife was a helpmate, an economic asset; children were economic assets after the age of five; there was less reason than now to defer marriage or to practice birth control.

5. The postponement of marriage and the limitation of the family have spread contraceptive knowledge and devices, removing the sanction of fear from the prohibition of extramarital relations.

6. Industrial competition among corporations and individuals has strengthened the profit motive and other individualistic instincts, and has broken down moral restraints in the conduct of business.

7. The wealth spawned by improved methods of production and distribution has enabled thousands of men and women to indulge in moral escapades that their ancestors could not afford.

8. Improvements in communication and transportation have given to local immorality and disorder a publicity that stimulates similar deviations elsewhere; and those improvements have facilitated the conspiracies of criminals and their flight from the scene of their crime.

9. The spread of education, while widening the classes that abstain from crime, has made the new generation increasingly familiar with the historical and geographical diversity of moral codes and their human origin; the inherited code has been thereby weakened, and much doubt has been cast upon its allegedly divine sanctions and source.

10. Technology has extended and depersonalized war, and has vastly developed man's ability to murder or destroy.

The character and frequency of modern war is second only to the Industrial Revolution as a cause of moral change. To fight such a war great numbers of young men are trained to use lethal weapons, and to kill with zest and a good conscience. The survivors, returning to civil life, keep some of the habits and temper of war, find it difficult to endure poverty amid surrounding wealth, and apply in the cities the techniques and principles learned in the camp and on the battlefield. The military class rises in prestige and influence, and its ways of thought, freed from moral considerations, affect the government and the people. Lying becomes a major industry of states. News and history are colored to inculcate hatred now of one enemy or competitor, now of another. Nationalism overrides morality, defers social reform, and becomes a religion stronger than any church.

From this résumé of old and familiar facts we conclude that morals would have changed even if religious beliefs had not been impaired by the conflict between religion and philosophy. Obviously the old moral code was adjusted to an agricultural society, and could not be expected to fit, without many alterations, the conditions of modern industrial life. Therefore we should speak of a moral change rather than a moral decay; the present age is experimenting, at its own peril, to find how far individual freedom can comport with the stability of society, the protection of women, and the security of person and property.

Such a transformation is bound to involve transitional chaos and some reckless extremes, but extremes often cancel themselves into moderation, and the chaos may compel new forms of discipline; the proposal for requiring two years of national service may be one of such forms, but it may also be the door to authoritarian government. As our young anarchists (barring a few congenital knights of the road) reach economic competence and place, and mature into intellectual perspective and some knowledge of the nature and limitations of man, they will probably adjust themselves to the discipline of industry and parentage; the radicals of today will become the liberals of tomorrow and the frightened conservatives of declining years. Which of us, if really alive, was not a rebel in his youth?

I am not sure, but I can reasonably hope, that as the United States has maintained a stable government for almost two centuries despite the separation of church and state, our industrial society will gradually develop a secular ethic that—with lessened poverty and widened education—will function as effectively as a theological morality. We must not imagine that past generations were much more moral than our own; the historian does not find them so, and the elders in every one of them thought them abandoned to Satan. Having freed ourselves from an oppressive hierarchy, we must not run away from our perilous liberty to seek mental quiet and asphyxiation in the womb of a loving but tyrannical Mother Church.

I have been reading with pride and amusement the argument that I made, in a little book published in 1917, for Socrates's view that intelligence is the highest virtue, and that education in intelligence can be made the basis of a natural morality. I must confess that I underestimated the role of sympathy—fellow feeling—in moral sentiments, as analyzed by David Hume and Adam Smith; and I realize that desire, instinct, and passion are the motive forces behind human behavior, even behind human reason. But I defined intelligence as the coordination of desires through a "forecasting of effects," and as delayed reaction allowing fuller perception of the situation and a more adequate response. Intelligence does not claim to be the source of action; it is the harmonious and effective unification of the sources.

Such intelligence is hard to teach, but it can be taught, in varying degrees, to differently developed minds. It does not seem impossible to make youth understand that the stability of a society, and the prevalence of moral restraint, are prerequisites to personal security, and that moral self-restraint is one of the surest guarantees of personal advancement and fulfillment. Actually crime and immorality, by and large, are least frequent in the best-educated ranks of a nation. Imagine what a natural ethic could do if as much time and care were spent in teaching it as the Church spends in inculcating a supernatural code. Let every grade in school, from kindergarten to PhD, have an hour per week of moral instruction, using a succession of textbooks of rising complexity from simple primers to mature treatises written by well-behaved philosophers, clergymen, and men of affairs, and rewritten by men allergic to preaching and gifted with clarity. Let such courses by humanized with readable biographies of moral leaders in thought and life: Confucius, Buddha, Socrates, Jesus, St. Francis of Assisi, Maimonides, Spinoza, Florence Nightingale, Schweitzer. I dream of all churches welcoming to their naves, an hour each week, all persons, of whatever theology or none, for discussion of practical ways in which human behavior, even in a secular world, could approach to the ideals of Christ. If more and more each new generation should receive more and more education it is reasonable to believe that morals would improve.

They will never satisfy the moralist, for morality is unnatural, goes against the grain; we are equipped by nature for a hunting life in woods and fields, rather than a mechanical life in cities, offices, and factories. But the problem of moral degeneration must be solved, for in the last analysis morality and civilization are one.

CHAPTER ELEVEN

ON MORALITY

I conclude from the foregoing disquisition that our moral "decay" is the natural if gradual dissolution of a once-puritan moral code that lost both its agricultural basis and rural environment, and that is slowly, with costly trial and error, evolving into a new code that is better adjusted to contemporary industry and technology, with a background of urban or suburban life, lengthened adolescence, smaller families, advanced education, religious doubt, free press, profuse publication, widened and accelerated communication and transport, and an unprecedented dissemination of comforts, opportunities, and wealth. These conditions have evoked revolutionary ventures, and youth has borne their brunt.

Before judging the revolt we should remind ourselves that it is the nature, function, and obligation of youth to rebel, as it is of old age to provide balancing resistance and checks, and of middle age to find some viable compromise between stability and liberty, stagnation and experiment. All things flow; the environment is always changing; old age, rooted in past conditions, is not equipped to meet external change with internal adjustments; youth, still incompletely formed, can add variation to heredity, innovation to imitation and tradition; and if it goes wrong it usually finds time to recover its footing. We older ones should be grateful that it is not our flesh and spirit that receive the blows and winds of change.

So, while I myself generally cling to the old code, I do not expect it of the young. I shudder at the shudders, convulsions, and bumps that make up their dances; I flee from their music and art as relics of the chaos that preceded creation; I close my ears to their four-letter words; and I wait impatiently for them to discover that Bohemianism, too, is a convention and a pose, and that their proud deviations from accepted manners reveal a secret doubt of their own inner worth. I counsel them to be as pure as Galahad, and I assure them that continence will do them no harm if they can buffet the taunts of sophomores shallow with sophistication. But I am not surprised that they do not take me seriously. I know that the widened gap between biological and economic maturity has put premarital sex relations into the new code.

The boy welling with hormones and coursing blood wonders why he should not solicit the cooperation of a similarly fretting girl in achieving detumescence. I warn him that such a pas de deux can plunge a generous and careless maiden into venereal infection, or to a pregnancy leading to a dangerous abortion, or to a hasty and regretted marriage, or to a career of complaisance that may win her nothing more permanent than a night's lodging; and I insist that a gentleman will refrain from coitus with any young lady whose social status and marital marketability would be injured by his passing triumph. I still believe it advisable to discourage extramarital relations, just as it is useful to inculcate honesty, though we know that there will be many lies.

Our forefathers could find no better way of promoting youthful continence than by adopting a policy of silence and concealment. This involved much hypocrisy, but it probably reduced the stimuli to erotic itching, it made premarital restraint more bearable, and it graced the relations of the sexes with a civilized courtesy and indirectness of action and speech that were among the charms of eighteenth-century society outside of the Squire Westerns. Today we adopt the other extreme: we throw a thousand suggestions of sex, normal and abnormal, into the face and mind of youth in cinemas, plays, periodicals, and books; and rare is the man who dares propose some restrictions upon this moneymaking liberty.

The modern exaltation of liberty has displaced parents from sharing in the choice of mates for their children. Lad and lass are left free to bind themselves till divorce or death, chiefly on the basis of the girl's physical charms magnified by the boy's erotic yearning (the girl contributes a touch of realism by considering the economic prospects of her suitor). As engagement in these days often involves sexual familiarity, and familiarity breeds indifference, many engagements are broken by youths free to seek new areas to explore. I believe that parents should alleviate the lengthened economic adolescence of their children by financing, at a regularly diminishing rate, the early years of marriage, but on condition that the children should agree not to marry without the consent of their parents. We must find some economic basis for restored parental authority.

I have a lingering inclination toward the Catholic view of divorce—that the annulment of a marriage should be allowed only under conditions of extreme personal or national need. (It was a costly error for Pope Clement VII to deny Henry VIII's plea for remarriage as necessary to begetting a male heir and insuring an orderly succession to the throne.) I believe that most divorces lead to difficulties as acute as before; we carry into a second union the same character that shared in breaking the previous bond. I admit that the steady confinement of two persons within the same house or cubicle—each facing the same face and décor day after day after day—is an unnatural strain on our powers of adjustment; but the easy sundering of a marital bond—with all the fragmentation of life that it implies, and all the psychological and economic disturbance it involves for the children—often brings more problems than it solves. Better to fight out the battle on the original field than run from one duel and surface to another. In the first case there is a reasonable chance that a compromise will be found, and that years of association, responsibility, and care will merge the combatants into a quiet but lasting love. Ariel and I have had many quarrels, but we have managed to patch them up in both life and letters; and after sixty-seven years we enjoy a delectable peace, and a mutual affection far deeper than youthful love.

It is an element of health in our moral life that today it is again fashionable to have children. I am not asking you to compound the overpopulation of the globe; three babies will meet your quota and will allow for one loss. Otherwise you may use any form of birth control that will not impair the health of your mate or yourself. Family limitation, of course, is unnatural, even through abstention, but so is any mode of locomotion except walking or running; civilization exists by checking nature at every turn. But don't contracept yourself out of the stream of life. Next to sharing the joys and sorrows of your spouse, the profoundest experiences of your career are the tribulations and delights given us by our children and their children. I count it as an unforgettable date in my life (July 2, 1946) when my grandson Jim, then four and a half years old, sitting in my lap, face to face, and feeling the fond embracement of my arms, surprised me with the tender assurance: "Even when you're dead you will remember how much you loved me."

Nothing can destroy my faith in our successors. I welcome their radical protests and revolts; we need and deserve them. We give our offspring twenty years of care and education and then conscript them for murder and death in foreign wars. We preach Christ to them and then cheat so much in business that the government has to intervene to protect the consumer against deceptive labels, dangerous cars, poisonous drugs, chemicalized food, and shoddy goods, while the government itself competes in corruption and mendacity.

By the side of our adult sins the absurdities of our children are merely the incidental measles of immaturity. Many features of their rebellion will succumb to the boredom of repetition. They will learn that four-letter words should be relegated to the gutter and the privy because by long association they smell of gutters and privies. Hallucinogenic drugs are enjoying a transient popularity, but I remember when my son Louis's generation at Cornell was eating goldfish and phonograph records. "Demonstrations" against war, economic abuses, and racial inequities are healthy; and it is a credit to both democracy and capitalism that no attempt has been made to suppress nonviolent critiques. However, I cannot admit the claim of many young enthusiasts that every person has a right to reject any law that his conscience finds unacceptable; no government could subsist on such a basis; the judgment of the community, as expressed by its elected legislators, rightly overrides the judgment of the individual. The individual may still carry legitimate protest to active disobedience, as Thoreau did, but he should take his punishment as due process of the law.

I mourn when brilliant writers like Andre Gide in his early works,[1] and some unfaithful followers of Freud, tell us that we should yield to every impulse and desire, and "be ourselves"! What jejune nonsense! Civilization, as Freud recognized and proclaimed, is at almost every moment dependent upon the repression of instincts, and intelligence itself involves discrimination between desires that may be pursued and those that should be subdued. For generations, youngsters, especially in America, have been misled by such reheated but half-baked philosophy.

I have left crime to the last in this personal assize of morals, because on this theme, especially, I can only repeat platitudes. Some crime may be ascribed to poverty, and to the displacement of manual labor by machinery. Some of its astonishing increase may be due to the disappearance of hell and the "death of God"; some of it to the decline of the family and parental authority. Some of it may derive from the circulation of psychoanalytic and philosophical nonsense, some of it from stories of crime in literature or on the screen. There is an anarchist in all of us that inclines us to sympathize with a felon who is desperately and cleverly eluding the police; nobody loves a policeman until he needs one. Part of crime's increase is due to new facilities for flight from a crime accomplished. Some of it may be debited to the liberal tendencies of our laws and courts: reacting against centuries of despotic government. Legislation since 1789 has been solicitous to protect the individual against the state; it is time our lawmakers should turn to protecting the community and the nation from malfeasance and crime. Our lawyers have proved too clever in finding legal technicalities and multiplying appeals to keep the criminal from his penalty. Latterly we have had too much freedom; we need some reassertion of authority in the home, the school, and the community. Reluctant though we are to meet the costs, we shall have to increase the number and pay, the training and equipment, of our detective forces and our police. An entire department of the government should be devoted to auditing the books, and examining the conduct, of every other branch of the government.

Capital punishment is unnecessary, but imprisonment for a major crime should not be easily abbreviated by wire-pulling parole, and we should not let murderers escape on pleas of "temporary insanity." We need not make our penal code a machinery of punishment and revenge; we should treat criminals as victims of mental disturbance or arrested development. Let us put them not in prisons that are nurseries and colleges of crime, but in securely enclosed state farms where steady labor in the open air could make for health and stability and accumulate a fund to finance the prisoner's reentry into civil life.

Suddenly all our civilization seems threatened by crime, war, racial strife, moral experiments, and urban decay. We pass these frightening problems on to our children, themselves so rootless and confused. If we can sustain our faith in education we may, by guiding the rising generations—white, black, and brown together—through school and college, generate the intelligence to meet these dangers, and to lift our lives to humane tolerance, orderly liberty, marital constancy, and an organized peace.

CHAPTER TWELVE

ON RACE

On the social aspect of this issue I should almost be an expert, for in a minor way I have been involved in the civil rights movement since 1914. In that year I began lecturing at Labor Temple (Fourteenth Street and Second Avenue, New York), where my audiences and friends included many minorities as well as a variety of whites. I was then in the habit of calling every person "brother," until it dawned upon me that there was something offensively patronizing in my use of that term. Soon after moving to Los Angeles (1943) I joined Meyer David in organizing a civil rights movement, which we called the Declaration of INTERdependence, arguing that nations and races and creeds must learn to work together or consume themselves in periodical strife. I believe it was my fervent pen that composed our proclamation of principles:

Human progress having reached a high level through respect for the liberty and dignity of men, it has become desirable to reaffirm these evident truths:

- *That differences of race, color, and creed are natural, and that diverse groups, institutions, and ideas are stimulating factors in the development of man;*
- *That to promote harmony in diversity is a responsible task of religion and statesmanship;*
- *That since no individual can express the whole truth, it is essential to treat with understanding and good will those whose views differ from our own;*
- *That by the testimony of history intolerance is the door to violence, brutality, and dictatorship; and*
- *That the realization of human interdependence and solidarity is the best guard of civilization.*

Therefore, we solemnly resolve, and invite everyone to join in united action:

- *To uphold and promote human fellowship through mutual consideration and respect;*
- *To champion human dignity and decency, and to safeguard these without distinction of race, or color, or creed;*
- *To strive in concert with others to discourage all animosities arising from these differences, and to unite all groups in the fair play of civilized life.*

Rooted in freedom, children of the same Divine Father, sharing everywhere a common human blood, we declare again that all men are brothers, and that mutual tolerance is the price of liberty.

And we had the luck to win to active association with us John Anson Ford, widely honored for his devotion and integrity as a member of the Los Angeles County Board of Supervisors, and Eric Scudder, whose keen mind, educated ear, and generous spirit soon raised him to prominence in law, music, and civic affairs. So strengthened, we arranged a dinner at which Thomas Mann spoke and Bette Davis took out of my amateur hands the raising of funds; and with this money we hired the Hollywood Bowl for a mass meeting on what we blithely called Interdependence Day, July 4, 1945.

Associate Justice Frank Murphy came from Washington to give the main address, and refused the $1,000 fee we offered him. A Catholic archbishop, a Protestant minister, a rabbi, and a black clergyman shared in the oratory; Protestant, Catholic, Jewish, and black choirs sang separately and then in unison; and I led the audience of eighteen thousand whites, blacks, Christians, and Jews in reciting the Declaration as a pledge taken before a justice of the Supreme Court. A year later the Board of Education agreed to place the Declaration in all the schools in Los Angeles and Mrs. H. David Kroll paid $1,000 to frame a thousand copies of the scroll. Now, we felt, we would go down in history on a level with Thomas Jefferson. Proud of its success and its eloquence, our little band rested on its oars, while racial chaos rose on every side.

Of course Meyer and I were innocent idealists, who had never looked into the depths of the racial caldron. We thought that an annual sermon and song would cool the heat that rises in our blood when we meet something strange and therefore dangerous. We had lived in the North, and had never felt the wounds of economic servitude, political disbarment, and social contumely. We had no conception of the white man's fear of black power growing in the North. We had underrated the spread and comfortable acceptance of propaganda proclaiming the inherent inferiority and limited educability of the black mind. We had never lived in a district where realty values had suffered from minority infiltration. We saw many successful black physicians, lawyers, clergymen, and office holders, and rejoiced in their mounting number and rapid advancement, but we had never felt the horror of a lynching, the humiliating rejection from hotels and restaurants, the hopeless poverty of Harlem or Watts. We lost ourselves in our individual tasks, and subsided into the unconscious satisfaction of belonging to the locally dominant race.

So, while I slowly grew up, the problem multiplied its forms, raised its hundred heads. In the South a black man might at any time be killed by a white man, who ran little risk of being convicted (if ever arrested) by a jury of his "peers"—i.e., all whites. A black person wishing to register as a voter was frustrated by a score of discriminatory requirements; and if he won and used the vote he would, as like as not, lose his job and the right to eat. A white man living in a predominantly black area was ready for any violence rather than let a black man rule the town; and white women trembled at the thought of being caught in strong black arms. So the South, so far as its need of manual laborers would permit, encouraged the black man to go north.

He went, dreaming of justice and plenty. For a time he found work where muscle was needed and servility was required; or he lived for a while on public aid, and alarmed the whites with his fertility. Thousands of Puerto Ricans poured into New York and helped to make it more colorful than ever; soon white children were in a minority in Manhattan's public schools. White families moved from New York, Boston, Philadelphia, Cleveland, and Chicago to the suburbs, leaving America's greatest cities darkened with new faces and new hates. Meanwhile the progress of technology deprived most black men of a place in industry; they became dependent upon relief, or charity, or their wives—who cleaned white homes to maintain black hovels. In crowded enclaves amid our wealth, poverty became race-colored and race-conscious, and drove men into a wild hostility that sanctioned any crime. The streets became unsafe. White citizens returned dislike for hate, and shrugged their shoulders at civil rights. Money voted for mitigating poverty went into the pockets of politicians, and distant war consumed the gold that had once been marked for the improvement of American life.

I should be a ridiculous upstart if I pretended to have solutions for all these problems. They rose out of the nature of man, which I cannot change with words. We distrust the unfamiliar, for we have not learned to deal with it; and when, in some moods and places, it speaks of burning us, we do not warm to the prospect.

This generation cannot solve the problem of unskilled labor left jobless by the progress of technology. We shall have to feed and house the sufferers, to retrain the educable, and to educate the children, until this generation passes away and the next has been prepared by our schools and colleges for a place in the new machinery of production, distribution, and finance. I believe that the nonwhite mind and character are as capable of improvement as any, provided that they have not been stunted by a hostile environment. To assure myself of this I need only look at the great number of nonwhites who have surmounted a thousand obstacles to reach excellence in literature, music, medicine, or law. So I make no apology for resorting again to my panacea—extended and expanded education.

The cynic will smile at this old-fashioned, eighteenth-century trust in education. But what is the alternative? It is a police state. It is a hundred years of internal hatred, social disorder, uncontrollable violence, and urban decay, just when the breakdown of geographical and communicative barriers subjects America to mounting, multiplying challenges by growing states and alien ideas. Do we not owe it to conscience and justice that every person—irrespective of their race—has full and equal opportunity to enter into the promise of American life?

CHAPTER THIRTEEN

ON WOMEN

L et me, before I die, sing a hymn in praise of women. Here Ariel, who is the First Cause of this paean, laughs at my ecstasy, and suggests that I should rather intone a song to my glands; beauty, she thinks, is in the eye of the gonads. Well, let us include the glands in our litany.

No one will believe me when I claim that I have often been aroused by the beauty of a woman without desiring her in any physical sense or degree; according to me my excitement was purely esthetic. Perhaps I deceive myself, and I will take no oath as to the lusts hiding in my "unconscious" or in my blood. But I insist that time and again I have longed to approach a woman timidly and thank her for being such a joy to behold, and that in this longing I felt no ambition to possess her, or even to touch her hand.

I am abnormally excited by any form of beauty; I am a nuisance to those who accompany me on my walks because I am always enthusing about something lovely or sublime—white clouds in a blue sky, or the honeyed fragrance of sweet alyssum, or the bright face of a passing youth, or the splendor of a tall, straight elm spreading its branches out as if in a Whitmanic cosmic embrace. When I think of how many beautiful things there must be on this dizzy planet I feel that I should be reconciled to immortality if I might see them all. But hardly anyone seems innocent or sentimental enough to join me in thanking whatever gods there be for creating or evolving woman.

I have read Schopenhauer on this dangerous subject, and I know that many of my contemporaries have spent volumes attacking these "vampires" who suck our life out with their charms and snares. In some lucid intervals I admit that many women have faults. Many are acquisitive, possessive, jealous, and proud. They are seldom capable of lasting friendships, since they must give so much time in winning, keeping, and giving love. Much of their beauty is artificial, and has to be laid aside before retiring. They are capable of stealing another woman's husband, breaking hearts, and breaking up homes. There are those that seldom think as objectively as some men; they are interested in ideas only so far as these are attached to interesting men; they often mistake wishes for facts, and repetitions for arguments; in some cases their vital force seems to skip their brains and exhaust itself in maintaining their luxuriant hair. They let themselves be fooled and gouged by couturiers who mistake novelty for beauty and who make a ninny of a woman for a price. They listen more readily than men to peddlers of supernatural hope and consolation, for their worries and grief are not so soon forgotten in the swift turmoil of the world. They give the race fewer geniuses than men do, but also fewer idiots. Intellect is sharpened in men by economic competition or political finagling; women do not need so much of it because they are normally destined to motherhood, in which instinct rules; and usually they win by instinct all that the male has acquired by intellect.

I put all the faults of woman aside because she is consumed and exalted in carrying on the race. Perhaps the race should not be carried on, but that is another question. I see her first as a girl, doubling her beauty with modesty, and vaguely, broodingly conscious that she is soon to be a hunted prey, then a fettered captive, then a racial tool. She has natural roses in her cheeks, for she takes actively to play and sport, to bicycles and horses; and she delights old eyes when she sits on the floor with her collie's head in her lap, and her still pretty feet bared to breathe the air.

My heart goes out to her as her adolescence nears its end, and I see young males gathering around her, anxious for her favor, eager for the touch of her hand, her lips, and plus ultra; I can imagine the winding, narrow road she must find between flirt and prude, between self-canceling conquests and intact solitude. No wonder if, as the prize of so many contests, she develops a preening vanity comparable to that of the sartorially meticulous male in the mating season. And what a burden is laid upon her in our time—to choose a suitor who does not stupefy her with adoration but, by his stability, restraint, and economic sense, gives promise of being a faithful husband, a competent provider, a sound and sane father for their children. What a responsibility to place upon this youthful brain and palpitating heart!

Now she is a bride, timid and proud, like a gambler who has staked his all on one throw of the dice or turn of the wheel. You might argue (if you have passed your climacteric) for the superiority of a racing horse with his gleaming coat and his nudging nose, or of your favorite dog, with his shapely head, his bounding grace, and his understanding eyes. I have had such moods, but come back to women—American, Irish, English, French, Spanish, Italian, German, Scandinavian, Polish, Russian (did you ever see Anna Pavlova?), Greek (we called our lovely guide in Greece in 1936 Aphrodite), Hindu, Muslim (have you read Arabic or Persian love poems?), Chinese, Japanese—they are all, even if so briefly, miracles of form, features, and alluring grace.

Almost anything about an educated woman in her prime can make me maudlin. I marvel at the velvet smoothness of her skin, the creamy softness of her hands, the delicate touch with which she strokes your face and lightens your purse. I would like to run my fingers through her hair, if that would not disturb its inviolable set. I dare not look into her eyes, for fear they will lure me into depths—if only of bathos—from which there is no return. Her voice tenderly lowered in love, or expertly raised in song, makes me wonder is not a god working in the laboratory of evolution. I think the architecture of woman is superb from whatever angle seen; I especially admire the frontal elevation, despite a tendency to weakness in support of overhanging masses. I take in stealthily the flashing of her ankles, the measured cadence of her nimble feet; but I resent the spikes that arm the nothings that she calls her shoes. The grace of her movement is poetry become flesh; I gape intoxicated at the fluid ease of her walk across the room, as if some silent and invisible zephyr made her weightless on her toes.

She becomes a mother. Now begin twenty or thirty years of worry and solicitude to make that child, and the next, and the next, healthy, decent, and intelligent. She bears the strain and stress of that process, in which she is a *dei genitrix*, a begetting, almost a goddess; if anywhere there is divinity it is here. No bi-

ologist could think of God except in feminine terms, for generally, in the world of life, the male is a tributary incident, usually
subordinate, sometimes superfluous. Catholics have been right
in praying chiefly to the mother of God. Many years ago, after
watching Ariel's pains in giving birth to Ethel Benvenuta, I left
the room dazed with shame at my helplessness, and mumbling
to myself: "I must always be kind to women." Let the sins of
woman lie gently on her head, for she is the forgiving mother
of us all.

A mother does not have to ask if life has any meaning;
when she sees her children growing in body and mind she
knows that she is fulfilling her destiny, and that her destiny is
fulfilling her. She will be rewarded when those children have
matured through the ills of childhood and the whims of youth
into men and women with offspring of their own. She will
gather that swelling brood about her, quietly proud and word-
lessly happy that they are the fruit of her body and soul; and
only a botched mind, seeing her loving them and loved by
them, would say that her life has no meaning. If life is lived
honorably and fully it is its own reward, needing no significance outside itself.

CHAPTER FOURTEEN

ON SEX

Why am I so infatuated with women? Why is it that now, in old age, I am almost as sensitive to feminine charms as when—while still a student in a Jesuit college, well over six decades ago—I stole away, now and then, to see a burlesque show? I again insist that in many instances the beauty of women arouses in me an esthetic emotion rather than any conscious desire. But that presumes a certain distance between us; if these entrancing females made the slightest advance I should be hard put to maintain the virginity of my thoughts. In general I presume that most men will react, almost by acquired reflex, to any sexual stimulus; and I have wondered considerably as to why we are such Pavlovian automata.

At times it has seemed to me that the physical attraction was due to concealment. Would the female bosom be an erotic spur if, as in old Bali, it had been perpetually exposed to male view? Concealment makes every revelation a thrilling gift. We might imagine that women, with their superior knowledge of sexual psychology, would husband their resources by cautious secrecy, as in Victorian days; instead, they have reached the judicious conclusion that partial veiling is better than none or all. Meanwhile male fancy is free to idealize those lovely protuberances, and to absolve them from all dependency upon time. Written or spoken words about them stir a curiosity that intensifies desire; and one wonders how much of our agitation is due to indoctrination. Was it La Rochefoucauld who asked, "Would anyone fall in love if he had never heard or read about such a delirium?"

In evolutionary theory those organisms that felt the strongest urge to mingle their seed bred most abundantly, so that, in the course of the generations, the sexual instinct grew to an intensity surpassed only in the quest for food. To a starving man Aphrodite might not appear as a paragon of beauty but only as a potential feast. However, when the basic quest has been satisfied, and man can turn his thoughts away from food and money, his soul lies open to all the lure and tyranny of sex. Consequently those nations—America, England, Germany, France—that have come closest to solving the problem of hunger are also those in which sex is most rampantly and irresponsibly free.

Nature (i.e., here, the evolutionary process) is mad about reproduction, and makes the individual a tool and moment in the continuance of the species. She cares little about anything but eating and begetting; all our literature, art, and music mean nothing to her except as stimulation or ornament to sex and continuity. In this perspective even eating is subordinate, however primary; it comes first, and without it life could not be; but it, too, is servant to sex; the unconscious purpose of our eating is to preserve and develop us for biological maturity—i.e., the ability to reproduce. When we have fulfilled that function we eat in order to survive as caretakers for our progeny. When we have completed both of these functions nature has no further use or regard for us; normally we would soon thereafter die; if we go on living it is as dispensable bystanders in the procession of life.

I can give no convincing reason why that procession should go on, but it will. Sometimes I resent the power that the sexual instinct has over us; I see it ruining lives, disordering states, making agitated apes of would-be philosophers; and I can understand why past civilizations have labored, by might and myth, to build dams against that swelling surge. The institution of marriage is a device to control the flow of that stream, whether by requiring monogamy in Christendom, or by allowing polygamy, and even concubinage, in Asia and Africa. In some Christian societies marriage is failing as such a dyke, and there is no telling whether Christian matrimony will be able to withstand the demands of the sexual instinct for greater freedom and wider variations.

I am not sure that I would want our sexual sensitivity to be reduced, for it is half the zest of life. Probably our sense of beauty is an offshoot of that sensibility; all other forms of beauty seem to be derived from the beauty of woman as the object of male desire and female envy; and perhaps the sense of sublimity has its primary source in female and male admiration of virile strength. To condemn sexual sensitivity would be to outlaw esthetic feeling and response, and so to cut the richest roots of art.

To find a pleasant medium between castration and erotic mania I must fall back upon my overburdened panacea—the development of intelligence. If we educate the body to health and the mind to a tempering harmony of instincts with reason, we shall retain the stimulus of sexual feeling while keeping it within bounds by a decent respect for public order, and a prudent foresight of our own good. It is quite possible to admire a hundred women or men while remaining resolutely faithful to one. In that way we may get the best of both boons—the transient ardor of sexual emotion and the quiet content of lasting love.

CHAPTER FIFTEEN

ON WAR

In the year 1830, a French customs official named Jacques Boucher de Crèvecœur de Perthes unearthed in the valley of the Somme some strange implements of flint now interpreted by the learned as the weapons with which the men of the Old Stone Age made war. These stones are called *coups de poing*, or "blows of the fist," for one end was rounded for grasping while the other was pointed for persuasion. With these modest tools of death, it seems, Neanderthal men, from what is now Germany, and Cro-Magnon men, from what is now France, fought fifty thousand years ago for the mastery of the continent, and, after a day of lusty battle, left perhaps a score of dead on the field. In the First and Second World Wars, modern Germans and modern Frenchmen fought again in that same valley, for that same prize, with magnificent tools of death that killed ten thousand men in a day. The art that has made the most indisputable progress is the art of war.

For five hundred centuries, two thousand generations have struggled for that terrain in a calendar of wars whose beginning is as obscure as its end. Even the sophisticated mind, made blasé by habituation to magnitude and marvels, is appalled by the panorama of historic war, from the occasional brawls and raids of normally peaceful "savages," through the sanguinary annals of Egypt, Sumer, Babylonia, and Assyria, the untiring fratricide of the Greek city-states, the conquests of Alexander and Caesar, the triumphs of Imperial Rome, the wars of expanding Islam, the slaughters of Mongol hordes, Tamerlane's pyramid of skulls, the Hundred Years' War, the Wars of the Roses, the Thirty Years' War, the War of the Spanish Succession, the Seven Years' War, the English, American, French, and Russian Revolutions, the Napoleonic Wars, the Civil War, the Franco-Prussian War, the Spanish-American War, the Russo-Japanese War, the First World War, the Second World War . . . This, to our pessimistic moments, seems to be the main and bloody current of history, beside which all the achievements of civilization, all the illumination of literature and art, all the tenderness of women and the chivalry of men, are but graceful incidents on the bank, helpless to change the course or character of the stream.

Such a chronicle of conflict exaggerates, without doubt, the role of war in the record of our race. Strife is dramatic, and (to most of our historians) peaceful generations appear to have no history. So our chroniclers leap from battle to battle, and unwittingly deform the past into a shambles. In our saner moments we know that it is not so; that lucid intervals of peace far outweigh, in any nation's story, the mad seizures of war; that the history of civilization—of law and morals, science and invention, religion and philosophy, letters and the arts—runs like hidden gold in the river of time.

Nevertheless, war has always been. Will it always be? What

are its causes in the nature of men and in the structure of societies? Can it be prevented, or diminished in frequency, or in
any measure controlled?

The causes of war are psychological, biological, economic,
and political—that is, they lie in the natural impulses of men,
in the competitions of groups, in the material needs of societies, and in the fluctuations of national ambition and power.

The basic causes are in ourselves, for the state is the soul of
man enlarged under the microscope of history. The major instincts of mankind—acquisition, mating, fighting, action, and
association—are the ultimate sources of war. For thousands,
perhaps millions, of years men were uncertain of their food
supply; not knowing yet the bounty of husbanded soil, they
depended upon the fortunes of the hunt. Having captured prey
they tore or cut it to pieces, often on the spot, and gorged
themselves to their cubic capacity with the raw flesh and the
warm gore; how could they tell when they might eat again?
Greed is eating, or hoarding, for the future; wealth is originally
a hedge against starvation; war is at first a raid for food. Perhaps
all vices were once virtues, indispensable in the struggle for existence; they became vices only in the degree to which social
order and increasing security rendered them unnecessary for
survival. Once men had to chase, to kill, to grasp, to overeat, to
hoard; a hundred millenniums of insecurity bred into the race
those acquisitive and possessive impulses which no laws or
morals or ideals, but only centuries of security, can mitigate or
destroy.

The desire for mates, and parental and filial love, write half
of the private history of mankind, but they have not often been
the causes of war. Probably the "rape of the Sabine women" was
the amorous result of a conflict for land and food.

The fighting instinct enters more obviously into the analysis. Nature develops it vigorously as an aid in getting food or mates; it arms every animal with organs of offense and defense, and lends to the physically weaker species the advantages of cunning and association. Since, by and large, those groups survived that excelled in food-getting, mate-getting, and fighting, these instincts have been selected and intensified through the generations, and have budded into a hundred secondary forms of acquisition, venery, and strife.

As the quest for food has expanded into the amassing of great fortunes, so the fighting instinct has swelled into the lust for power and the waging of war. The lust for power is in most men a useful stimulus to ambition and creation, but in exceptional men it can become a dangerous disease, a cancer of the soul, which goads them on to fight a thousand battles, usually by proxy. Nietzsche, nervous and sickly, disqualified for military service, thrilled at the sight and sound of cavalry galloping along a Frankfurt street, and at once composed a paean in honor of war and the "will to power."

The instinct of action enters into the picture as a love of adventure, or escape from relatives or routine. A wider source is the instinct of association. Men fear solitude, and naturally seek the protection of numbers. Slowly a society develops within whose guarded frontiers men are free to live peaceably, to accumulate knowledge and goods, and to worship their gods. Since our self-love overflows, by an extension of the ego, into love of our parents and children, our homes and possessions, our habits and institutions, our wonted environment and transmitted faith, we form in time an emotional attachment for the nation and the civilization of which these are constituent parts; and when any of them is threatened, our instinct of pugnacity is aroused to the limit demanded by the natural cowardice of mankind. In a divided and lawless world such patriotism is reasonable and necessary, for without it the group could not survive, and the individual could not survive without the group. Prejudice is fatal to philosophy, but indispensable to a nation.

Put all these passions together—gather into one force the acquisitiveness, pugnacity, egoism, egotism, affection, and lust for power of a hundred million souls, and you have the psychological sources of war. Take them in their mass, and they become biological sources. The group, too, as well as the individual, can be hungry or angry, ambitious or proud; the group, too, must struggle for existence, and be eliminated or survive. The protective fertility of organisms soon multiplies mouths beyond the local food supply; the hunger of the parts, as in the body, becomes the hunger of the whole, and species war against species, group against group, for lands or waters that may give more support to abounding life. Euripides, twenty-three hundred years ago, attributed the Trojan War to the rapid multiplication of the Greeks.

Group hunger begets group pugnacity, and pugnacity develops in the group, as in the individual, organs of protection and attack. In the group these are called armament; and when they are powerful, they may themselves, like the boy's consciousness of his biceps, become a secondary source of war. On either scale some armament is necessary, for struggle is inevitable, and competition is the trade of life.

These psychological and biological forces are the ultimate origins of human conflict. From them flow the national rivalries that generate the proximate causes of war—those economic and political causes with which superficial analysis so readily contents itself.

The basic economic cause is rivalry for land: land to receive a designedly expanding population, land to provide material resources, land to open up new subjects to conscription and taxation. So the ancient Greeks spread through the Aegean, the Black Sea, and the Mediterranean to Byzantium, Ephesus, Alexandria, Syracuse, Naples, Marseilles, and Spain; so the English spread through the world in the last two centuries; and so the Americans are spreading now.

These standard provocations to conquest have been sharpened and magnified by the Industrial Revolution. To make war successfully, a modern nation must be wealthy; to be wealthy it must develop industry; to maintain industry, it must, in most cases, import food, fuel, and raw materials; to pay for these, it must export manufactured goods; to sell these, it must find foreign markets; to win these, it must undersell its competitors or wage foreign war. As like as not, it will make war for any of the goods it considers vital, or for control of the routes by which they must come.

Greece fought for control of the Aegean, the Hellespont, and the Black Sea, because it was dependent upon Russian grain. Rome had to conquer Egypt because it needed corn, and Asia Minor because it needed markets for its handicrafts and fortunes for its politicians. Egyptian wheat, Near Eastern oil, and Indian cotton explain many a battle in British history; Spanish silver explains the wars of Rome with Carthage; Spanish copper has something to do with German aid to Fascist Spain. Our sinless selves had a taste for sugar in 1898; and far back in 1853 we pointed our gifts and cannon at a Japanese government and persuaded Japan to transform itself into an industrial nation eager for foreign markets and spoils. These Japanese chickens came home to roost at Pearl Harbor in 1941.

The business cycle adds its own contribution to the causes of modern war. Since men are by nature unequal it follows that in any society a majority of abilities will be possessed by a minority of men; from which it follows that sooner or later, in any society, a majority of goods will be possessed by a minority of men. But this natural concentration of wealth impedes, by the repeated reinvestment of profits in promoting production, widespread purchasing power among the people; production leaps ahead of consumption; surpluses rise and generate either depression or war. For either production must stop to let consumption catch up, or foreign markets must be found to take the surplus that was unpurchased at home.

Add a few political causes of war. The first law of governments is self-preservation; their second law is self-extension; their appetite grows by what it feeds on, and they believe that when a state ceases to expand it begins to die. Furthermore, the distribution of power among nations is always changing through the discovery or development of new processes or resources, through the rise or decline of population, through the weakening of religion, morals, and character, or through some other material, biological, or psychological circumstance; and the nation that has become strong soon asserts itself over the nation that has become weak. Hence the difficulty of writing a peace pact that will perpetuate a present arrangement. Wonderful indeed is the treaty that does not generate a war. Peace is war by other means.

If the foregoing analysis is substantially correct, we must not expect too much from those who seek to end or mitigate war. William James, in his kindly way, hoped that the enrollment of the nation's youth, for a year or two, in a far-flung "War against Nature" would give creative expression to the impulses of action, adventure, and association, and so provide a "moral equivalent for war"; America is trying this in its excellent Peace Corps; but obviously such measures do not reach to the major sources of international strife. The League of Nations (except under Briand and Stresemann) was a conspiracy of the victors to preserve their gains; it had to fail as soon as the fertility and industry of the defeated had altered the balance of national power prescribed by the Treaty of Versailles. The life of nations cannot be straightjacketed into immutability. Pacifism would be a cure for war if it could survive the call to arms and national defense; the same English youth that had, in the Oxford Union, vowed never to take up arms for England, took them up manfully against Hitler.

Vague appeals to the conscience of mankind to put an end to war have had little effect throughout history, for there is no conscience of mankind. Morality is a habit of order generated by centuries of compulsion; international morality awaits international order; international order awaits international force; conscience follows the policeman. A wise people will love peace and keep its powder dry.

An effective approach to the problem of war will proceed, not by large and generous emotions, but by the specific study and patient adjustment of specific causes and disputes. Peace must be planned and organized as realistically as war—with provision for every factor, and prevision for every detail. This cannot be done in an occasional moment stolen by statesmen from internal affairs; it requires the full-time attention of first-rate minds. The incentives to war are so numerous and powerful that each of them should be the major concern of an international commission specifically appointed for its consideration and adjustments. There are so many specialists, economists, and diplomats lying around (to use this verb in a purely physical sense) that we might well distribute them into commissions severally assigned to examine the economic causes of war, to hear the disputing groups patiently, to investigate possibilities of conciliation, to make specific and practicable recommendations to their governments, and to do their work without the explosive excitement of publicity. We must isolate the germs of war at their source, and sterilize them with understanding and negotiation.

One such commission would study the problems generated by reckless human fertility. It could promote policies and methods of family limitation wherever the birthrate (minus the death rate) is outrunning the visible or prospective means of subsistence; it would prepare international procedures for mitigating local shortages of food; it would seek territorial outlets for the expansion of congested populations. A permanent commission might study the access of industrial nations to material, fuels, and markets. It should be a major function of the Department of State to wage peace vigorously and continuously on every front.

In the end we must steel ourselves against utopias and be content, as Aristotle recommended, with a slightly better state. We must not expect the world to improve much faster than ourselves. Perhaps, if we can broaden our borders with intelligent study, impartial histories, modest travel, and honest thought—if we can become conscious of the needs and views and hopes of other peoples, and sensitive to the diverse values and beauties of diverse cultures and lands, we shall not so readily plunge into competitive homicide, but shall find room in our hearts for a wider understanding and an almost universal sympathy. We shall find in all nations qualities and accomplish-ments from which we may learn and refresh ourselves, and by which we may enrich our inheritance and our posterity. Some-day, let us hope, it will be permitted us to love our country without betraying mankind.

CHAPTER SIXTEEN

ON VIETNAM

Anything written on May 7, 1967, about so fluent a situation as the war in Vietnam will almost certainly seem foolish in 1969; even the pronouncements of the best-informed statesmen have provided some wry humor in a year or two. But I stand up to be counted; I speak my piece, and take my chance with sardonic time.

It is one distinction of the twentieth century that while protests against war have mounted, war has become more frequent and extensive, more destructive of life and property, than ever before. Poets, philosophers, and mothers mourn, but our instincts continue to divide mankind into jealous or hostile races, nations, classes, and creeds. The possession of power tempts to its use; the definition of national interest widens to cover any aim; the demand for security suggests and excuses the acquisition and arming of ever more distant frontiers. Men above military age are readily moved by calls to patriotism; pleaders for peace are scorned as cowards, and arguments for mutual understanding and adjustment are branded as appeasement—

as if to appease a quarrel were to sin against the Holy Ghost. The organs of public opinion are conscripted to expound and exalt the generals; a soldier's uniform transfigures a civilian, intoxicates a maiden, and almost reconciles a mother to the killing of her son. Governments find it easier to begin a war than to win an election.

The Constitution of the United States reserves to Congress the right to declare war, but it does not forbid the president to wage war if he can call it by another name. This may sometimes be made necessary by international crisis requiring quick action—which might not be obtainable from a deliberative assembly. In effect, as regards war and peace, the American presidency is a dictatorship limited in time, allowing impotent public criticism, and ultimately guided by generals and admirals. Armed with this strategy, American presidents have repeatedly initiated military intervention in foreign states, and Congress, faced by an accomplished fact, has felt compelled to approve.

In 1948 the Sixth Fleet of the United States was ordered to prevent a Communist revolt in Greece, and to resist Russian pressure upon Turkey. In 1957 Congress sanctioned the Eisenhower Doctrine, which pledged the United States to aid any Middle East nation threatened by "overt armed aggression from any country controlled by International Communism" (*Los Angeles Times*, May 1, 1957); on this basis help was given to the government of Jordan, and American troops were landed in Lebanon (1958), although "in neither instance was there real evidence of 'overt' aggression from a Communist-controlled country" (ibid). President Kennedy reaffirmed the Eisenhower Doctrine in 1963. In 1965 President Johnson declared that the financial and military power of his country would be used, at the request of any Asiatic government, to suppress any revolutionary movement suspected of communistic inclinations.

These pronouncements were not made without provocation. Communist leaders in Russia and China had explicitly and repeatedly declared their resolve to overthrow the American economic system, and to foment and support "wars of liberation" for the establishment of Communist governments in non-Communist states. Since nearly every revolutionary movement has in our time a Communist tinge, the United States stands committed to send its troops to sit on the lid of any simmering pot. Wherever an impoverished people rises in protest against economic exploitation or political tyranny, we are pledged, on request from an endangered government, to suppress the revolt. (We are not pledged to aid an elected government which is attacked by a conservative army.) We announce to the poor of the world that the Communist states are their friends and we are their enemies. The United States, which was born of a revolution, becomes, all by itself, another Holy Alliance, like that which Metternich, in 1815, dedicated to the suppression of every revolutionary movement in Europe. Was this a part of the American dream?

Let us put the best interpretation upon this new view of America's role in history. We imagine some State Department official speaking:

> The United States, having saved Western Europe from Hitlerian abominations and Slavic domination, sees its friends and allies in the Far East faced with the expanding power of Communist China. Great Britain is no longer able to finance its old role of protecting the rights, interests, and civilization of the white man in Asia. If no other power undertakes this role the

numerical superiority of the foreign races, added to their rabid adoption of Western technology, inevitably entails the subordination of Western Europe and America to a spreading coalition of Asia and Africa. Unless immediate and effective resistance is made to the extension of Chinese power the white man is doomed to second-class status in the world of the twentieth century. Step by step Chinese ascendancy will be established in Southeast Asia—in Cambodia and Laos, in Vietnam and Thailand, in Indonesia, Malaysia, and Singapore. Thereafter, Taiwan, the Philippines, perhaps even Japan, will be at the mercy of the multiplying, nuclear-armed Chinese. That these dangers are real is shown by the report that "non-Communist countries of Southeast Asia appear to be more confident about their future as a result of the United States' stand in Vietnam and the political convulsions in Peking" (New York Times, April 30, 1967, 1). Furthermore, Australia and New Zealand will have to be defended against strangulation by the Chinese dragon, or they will have to allow their governments and their way of life to be transformed by foreign immigration and dominance.

We are not asserting the inherent superiority of the white man to men of different races; it happens that we are white, and feel an obligation to defend our like, even though they may have made mistakes and committed sins in the past. We need not stress the fact that through such an extension of Chinese power Western Europe and America would lose their Oriental allies, markets, supplies, commercial facilities, and trade routes. Western Europe would be thrown back upon its own natural resources for materials and fuels, which are already inadequate. Communist parties would be strengthened in Italy and France, perhaps to the point of capturing the government. Latin Amer-

ica would be flooded with Communist agents organizing one revolution after another. Finally, shorn of its allies, the United States would be enveloped in a Communist sea.

Granting that these fears may be exaggerated, is it not wiser for America to meet the danger at the outset, and to fight it out on foreign soil, rather than wait for the problem to be doubled and trebled by delay, while we sit supine until the enemy is at our doors? We know the natural reluctance of our people to send their sons to distant battlefields for a purpose visible only to farseeing minds; but what would our grandchildren think of us if they found themselves encircled and commanded by alien powers because of our short sight, procrastination, and cowardice? We must think in terms of generations and centuries.

It is a powerful argument, and I can in some degree appreciate the spiritual loneliness and angry resolution of the president who has determined to follow it to the bloody end though it may cost him the love of his people, and the failure of his grand design to abolish poverty and racial injustice in America. I resent the hysterical and indecent abuse heaped upon him by those who reject his policies without facing his problems and responsibilities. I know that he has given his life to understanding political affairs whose arcana are concealed from an ivory-tower recluse like me. But though I have lost so much of my religious faith, I remain (even after reading a dozen volumes of Nietzsche) unconvertibly an *anima naturaliter Christiana* and I treasure the words of a lovable Galilean who wished "to preach glad tidings to the poor, . . . to preach deliverance to captives, . . . to set the downtrodden free" (Luke 4:18).

I am less inspired by calls to establish an American Empire, with military outposts and stockpiles five thousand miles away from its continental frontiers, or by a policy containing the seeds of countless wars, than I am by the hope that somewhere, sometime, it will be permitted us to behave like Christians, or like gentlemen, even to the stranger at the gate. I believe it would have been cheaper, as well as more human, to export food and technical aid to impoverished areas, to advise threatened governments to become welfare states, to prod the great landowners in those countries to allow a wider distribution of land, to persuade industrial magnates that higher wages make for expanding markets, rising profits, economic stability, and political peace.

Long ago, repeatedly and publicly (e.g., in the *New York World-Telegram* of September 19, 1961), I urged that despite its Communist revolution—which the nature of man will make a transient incident in a long history—China should be recognized as a civilization, rich in annals of statesmanship, moral philosophy, literature, and art; that we should be patient with its turmoil, hold out to it the hand of friendship, and facilitate, instead of opposing, its entry into the United Nations. I still think this would have been better for the political and military—if not for the oratorial—peace of the world. I have felt that international order would have been furthered if America had resolutely held back from expansion, and, by a reverse Monroe Doctrine, had pledged herself not to interfere in the politics of any nation on the Asiatic mainland. I was, and am, convinced that an offer of fair and candid negotiations with China, stipulating the security of Australia and New Zealand, could not have had worse results than a policy of mutual misunderstanding, misrepresentation, hatred, and war. Instead we have passionate enemies, for generations to come, of the most populous nation—soon to be one of the most powerful nations—in the world. We have left to our children this legacy of hate, presaging world conflicts involving a billion men.

I do not need to be told that Machiavelli, and a thousand statesmen before or after him, have denied the practicability of applying to the conduct of governments the restraints laid upon individuals by codes of morals and laws. I know that political practitioners have implied—often by their deeds, sometimes by frank words—that a government must feel free to lie, steal, and kill whenever in its judgment this is required by the national interest. I admit that a government which, in its dealings with other states, observed the Ten Commandments and the Golden Rule, would run great risk of having these rules ignored by its enemies; and that in such a case there would be no effective superior power to appeal to, as an injured and innocent citizen may appeal to his country's laws. I admit that the United Nations, through the vetoes allowed in its Security Council, and the unrealistic numerical organization of its General Assembly, offers no practical machinery for deciding issues between Great Powers; and that in no major states is public opinion ready to abandon national sovereignty. But we had a right to expect that our government would sign the Geneva Agreements of 1954, guaranteeing a neutral Vietnam; and that our economic interests there would be left to negotiation rather than to escalated interference and war. I would rather have America lose her empire than have her forfeit all the inspiration that she has meant to mankind.

Even now I would like to see our president offer to Ho Chi Minh, and to the Viet Cong, with the consent of the South Vietnamese Government, proposals for (1) a month's cessation, by both sides, of all offensive military action or advance (military preparation cannot be checked or prevented); (2) a free election of a new government in South Vietnam by all South Vietnamese adults, under neutral surveillance; (3) recognition of the Viet Cong as a participant in the negotiations and in the new government; (4) gradual withdrawal of American military forces from South Vietnam after the establishment of an elected government capable of maintaining order; (5) pledge of extensive aid to repair the damages of war, and to encourage a progressive economy, in all Vietnam, North as well as South.

I have no delusion that the president will listen to a tender-minded tenderfoot sitting on a California hill and mourning the daily crucifixion of Christ. Events have moved so rapidly, and the decisions of three administrations have so involved us, that the majority of Americans seem reconciled to pursue the policy of force to its incalculable and possibly cataclysmic end. But keep on hoping (for hope is the staff of life) that our children may learn something from this costly lesson, and be brave enough, despite whatever contumely, to try peace and friendship instead of hate and war, and so restore the America that we loved in our youth.

CHAPTER SEVENTEEN

ON POLITICS

In preparing these chapters I have often looked into my 1929 ebullition, *The Mansions of Philosophy*, to avoid repeating old sallies and arguments. Sometimes I paused in admiration of my youthful eloquence (I was only forty-four, which is childhood in philosophy). But one chapter shocked me as the most one-sided, unfair, and immature disquisition that ever came from my pen.

It was entitled "Is Democracy a Failure?" And it described with enthusiasm all the faults of democracy in America: its dependence upon a public opinion misinformed, misled, and thoughtlessly passionate; its nominations controlled by political machines favoring obedient mediocrities; its municipal officialdom corrupt and incompetent; its legislatures and Congress subservient to lobbies and wealth; its leaders too busy with electioneering to have time to think. My nostrum for these ills was the establishment, in our universities, of accredited schools of administration, diplomacy, and government; the automatic right of any graduate of such a school to present himself as a candidate for municipal office; the automatic eligibility to state office of any graduate after serving two terms as mayor of a state's largest city; the automatic eligibility to Congress of any graduate after serving two terms as governor; and the automatic eligibility for the presidency or vice presidency of any graduate after serving two terms as senator. Party and machine nominations would continue, and would be open to all, regardless of fitness, but education would no longer be a disqualification for office; and even the parties might now and then nominate a man as specifically trained for public administration as a student is trained for the practice of medicine or law. I still cherish this nicely graduated scheme, and I rejoice to note how many universities have organized schools of government. But, for the rest, I repudiate that early article as a shameful outburst of ingratitude and spleen. (I shiver to imagine what I should think of the present essay if by some mischance I should live to reread it many years hence.)

Since 1929 American democracy has matched its defects with its achievements. It has raised the quality of its mayors, governors, and presidents: Franklin Roosevelt, Fiorello La Guardia, John Lindsay, and Nelson Rockefeller have inspired us with their courage, integrity, and vision. The national government has met the challenges of depression, racial crisis, and two world wars. It has often been far ahead of public opinion in measures that later won general acclaim. It has made almost as many concessions to labor as to business; it has begun to protect borrowers from usurers, and purchasers from false packaging or labeling. And it has saved the American economy by mitigating capitalistic rigors with the welfare state.

I know that the welfare state is distrusted by many sincere conservatives as biologically unsound; men, they believe, are naturally averse to labor, and need the fear of hunger or want as a prod to work. Some critics would add that poverty is mostly due to native inferiority in body, mind, or character rather than to inequities in the relations between employers and employees; a few would secretly agree with Nietzsche that the poor are the social organism's natural waste, and we must stoutly resign ourselves to its unseemly necessity. We recall Macaulay's warning that democracy would collapse when the poor used their electoral power to rob rich Peter to pay lazy Paul. Polybius expressed the same idea in 130 BC:

> When, by their foolish thirst for reputation, they [popular leaders] have created among the masses an appetite for gifts and the habit of receiving them, democracy in its turn is abolished, and changes into a rule of force and violence. . . . For the people, having grown accustomed to feed at the expense of others, and to depend for their livelihood on the property of others, . . . degenerate into perfect savages, and find once more a master and monarch.[1]

So the Greek historian, following Plato, thought that democracy would by its own excesses pass into dictatorship.

The danger is real. I admit that thousands of people use pensions, relief checks, and unemployment benefits to finance long periods of indolence; that many employees live apart from their wives and children in order that these may be eligible for relief; and that voluntary idleness at public expense has become a drain on municipal, state, and national treasuries, which are maintained by ever-rising taxation. Nevertheless, the welfare state must be preserved and extended (in this matter we are far behind the British), not only as a dictate of decency but as a measure of insurance against class conflict at home and foreign competition for the suffrages of mankind.

It is to the honor of the American economy that it can flourish only if the power of the people to purchase goods rises step by step with their power to produce them; and production is repeatedly advanced by improved technology, management, and skills.

We have elsewhere argued that all men are born unequal; that these natural inequalities grow with time and the complexity of productive techniques; that the consequently concentrated wealth is mostly invested in mechanizing and accelerating production; that the gap between production and consumption widens until production slows to let consumption catch up. But the retarding of production lowers the total of wages paid, still further widens the gap between wealth and poverty, and threatens the existence of the free enterprise system. The cheapest alternative to this vicious spiral is an ampler distribution of the wealth generated by the zest and stimulations of capitalism. From 1933 to 1965 the government of the United States achieved this by encouraging the organization and bargaining power of labor, by extending the graduated tax on incomes and estates, and by payments from the treasury to promote public health, security, education, recreation, and employment; i.e., by extending the welfare state. Next to the brilliant repulse of Fascist Germany and imperialistic Japan, this has been the most vital achievement of American statesmanship in our time.

Largely for these reasons I have, since 1916, favored the Democratic as against the Republican Party, except that in 1928 I supported Herbert Hoover. As an aging cub reporter for the Scripps-Howard newspapers at the Democratic Convention in that year I was captivated by the handsome presence and buoyant spirit of Franklin Roosevelt, who there nominated Alfred Smith; and I suggested that the Convention would show good sense if it nominated the nominator rather than his religion-hobbled nominee. Of course no one listened to me, but I had my way in 1932, and I voted for Roosevelt as long as he lived. I rank him among our greatest presidents. He rescued democracy abroad by coming to the aid of France and England in 1941; he rescued democracy at home by making government the instrument of the common weal instead of the servant of capital. Because of him and his successors the American system was so chastened and strengthened that it has been able to meet every challenge and comparison. The grandchildren of our tycoons will build statues to him.

The war against poverty is in its early stages; it is an immense and unprecedented enterprise; it is entitled to make mistakes. It is handicapped by the growth of ghettos in our cities and of racial animosities in our hearts. In these respects Western Europe is more fortunate than the United States. Its cities are better managed by officials better trained, its traditions of social order are more deeply rooted in time and character, and its unassimilated ethnic minorities are relatively small. I have been appalled, on my annual visits to New York, to see how foreign immigration, white emigration, and the differential birthrate are conspiring to make our leading city a confusion of poor foreign people surrounding poor white enclaves, amid a forest of hotel or office towers possessed by proud suburbanites who enter in the morning and flee in the afternoon. Are our great cities doomed to race hatreds, class war, and relief expenditures threatening municipal bankruptcy? How shall we ever absorb these hostile millions into American life?

We shall do it by passing their children and grandchildren

through our schools and colleges, through our political institutions, and through the training of skills in an "equal opportunity" economy. For a decade or more there will be suspicion, resentment, disorder, violence, but these will subside. Over a century ago, when the Know Nothing Party and its riots inflamed America, it was dangerous to be a Catholic; now in many of our cities it is dangerous not to be a Catholic. In my youth the Italians in America were digging ditches; today Italians control the largest bank in the United States. Consider the progress made by the American Jews in the last half-century: in my youth I knew them as the harassed and impoverished people of the Lower East Side in New York; now I know their descendants as forming one of the most numerous, affluent, and respected elements in Los Angeles. History does not forbid us to hope for a similar rise of our darker-skinned brothers and sisters. The melting pot still melts, though not so much by mingling bloods as by raising the level of education and the standard of life. The process has been retarded by color differences and excessive immigration; and yet there are hundreds of thousands of prosperous minorities in the United States today. How many more will there be after another half-century of universal free schooling, and widened access to positions that develop intelligence and responsibility?

I have followed with care the helpful criticisms that others have made of our educational system. My own estimate of it derives from no systematic study but from experience as a teacher in a public school, a private school, a college, and a university—all, however, before 1938. I believe that European schools and colleges give the student a better training than ours do in knowledge, thinking, and discipline of character and mind. But I count not on the superiority of our schools so much as upon their number and reach. I see them responding to criticism, checking their laxity, paring their frills, and raising the mental level and equipment of a whole people, including racial minorities. It is a heroic enterprise, facing apathy, prejudice, and a taxpayers' revolt; but when I am driven to my last stand I place my faith in the courage of our people, and our educational institutions, to justify America in history.

I know the defects of democracy; I have too readily advertised and condemned them. I know also, through history and travel, the other forms of government. I have read of Louis XIV, his gorgeous robes and the grandeur of Versailles; but behind that costly façade I have seen the dehumanized peasants described in the most famous pages of La Bruyère. I have no wish to exchange Moscow or Peking for Washington or Los Angeles. I believe that ability has more abundant opportunities to reach maturity and influence in our democracy than under aristocracies or monarchies—or under democracies still obstructed by aristocratic privilege. I am grateful for the freedom of mind that I have enjoyed in America; I do not think I should have found so wide and open a road in any other land.

I recognize that many evils tarnish our record—aggressive war, childish chauvinism, political corruption, business chicanery, racial inequities, proliferating crime, broken marriages, declining morals, and decadent arts. Nor do I expect that the nature of man will change to remove the biological sources of our sins and ills. Against these woes the cries of our pessimists are justified and useful. But I see the best as well as the worst, and I will not apologize for my country. If the Founding Fathers could come back they would be amazed at the degree to which we have reduced poverty, drudgery, illiteracy, and governmental tyranny. A large part of the utopias described by

Thomas More, Samuel Butler, Edward Bellamy, and H. G. Wells has been materially realized, along with the universal education, adult suffrage, freedom of speech, press, assembly, and religion which were among the hopes and dreams of eighteenth-century philosophers.

Let us continue to complain, to demand, and to rebel; this, too, is part of our virtue. But as for me, favored and fortunate (and countless Americans might say the same), I should be the worst ingrate if I did not thank the fates that deposited me here between these seas, and within these liberties.

ON CAPITALISM
AND COMMUNISM

W hy do we become more conservative as we age? Is it because we have found a place in the existing system, have risen to a larger income, and have invested our savings in an economy, which any significant revolt might alter to our loss? I believe this is the primary cause. But we should admit a secondary cause, which conservatives hold to be fundamental: a growing knowledge of human nature, and of the limits that human behavior puts upon the attainment of ideals. Presumably there is also a physiological cause—a lessening of vital forces as the years advance.

My own passage from devout radicalism to cautious liberalism may illustrate the transition, and may allow the reader to discount my conclusions. I have told this story elsewhere, I summarize it here. Raised in a Roman Catholic family of confirmed Republicans, I leaped in a year (c. 1905, aged nineteen) into agnosticism and socialism. I entered a Catholic seminary in 1909 in the delusion that I might, as a priest, influence the

Church to support socialist ideas. In 1911 I left the seminary, and became the sole teacher and chief pupil in the Ferrer Modern School in New York. The school had been named after a martyred Spanish rebel against Church control of schools in Spain, and was managed by a board of anarchists and socialists led by Emma Goldman, Alexander Berkman, Harry Kelly, and Leonard Abbott. Emma Goldman was a doctrinaire and authoritarian apostle of liberty. Berkman was a sincere and lovable unionist who, at the age of twenty-two, tried to kill Henry Clay Frick (1892), head of the Carnegie Steel Company; deported to Soviet Russia in 1919, he left it as the contrary of his ideal, lived in France in disillusionment and despair, and killed himself in 1936. Harry Kelly was a tireless devotee, who opposed the printing of an article by me in the magazine *Mother Earth* on the ground that I followed a socialist rather than an anarchist line; I learned then that rebels have the same instincts as other people, without the caution that keeps others in line. Leonard Abbott was a highly cultured "philosophical anarchist," whose belief in liberty and rebellion was tempered by an open mind and a generous spirit; we called him, in no financial sense, "the angel of the radical movement." He was one of the finest human beings that I have known.

I remained a socialist from 1905 till 1916, when I betrayed the faith by working for the reelection of Woodrow Wilson. A socialist daily, the *New York Call*, branded my apostasy with a pungent editorial entitled "We Know This Breed." I joined Amos Pinchot's "Wilson Volunteers," who barnstormed New York State. Walter Lippmann, who had already (1916) made his mark as a political philosopher, addressed major gatherings in halls or theaters; I spoke to small groups in the streets. Wilson lost the state.

My socialist sympathies survived that election, and were re-kindled by the Russian Revolution (1917), which I hailed as a blessing for all mankind. This faith endured till 1932, when Ariel and I traveled through Siberia and European Russia; there we saw not Utopia but chaos, regimentation, brutality, and starvation; we came back so disillusioned that we have never been quite the same again. I wrote in haste some magazine articles, which I gathered into a little book, *The Tragedy of Russia* (1933); they lost me a host of friends among the radicals and literati of New York.

Of course I judged Russia foolishly in 1932. Despite my addiction to history I failed to interpret those awful conditions in the light of the past. I forgot that Russia, for hundreds of years, had known bitter exploitation and poverty; that it had just waged and lost a war which had shattered the order and economy of the nation; that the new state had had to spend its surviving human and material resources in fighting off enemies and former allies on a dozen fronts from Germany to Japan; and that fifteen years were not enough to beat all that chaos into order, or to transform that agony and starvation into plenty and content. I could not realize that in the economic disarray of 1917, the general illiteracy, and the collapse of local and central government, a peaceful and operative democracy would have been impossible. Russia in 1917–32 was a nation at war, surrounded and besieged, threatened with conquest and disintegration. It did what any nation so situated would have to do: it put democracy aside as a luxury of order, security, and peace, and set up a dictatorial regime as the sole alternative to disaster. Communism in those years was a war economy, such as we ourselves may have to resort to in the next world war; and perhaps its continuance depended upon the persistent threat and fear of war.

Meanwhile that once merciless dictatorship startled the world with its accomplishments. In fifty years it had made Russia one of the strongest nations on earth. Despite droughts, starvation, revolts, purges, and concentration camps, and a thousand mistakes of economic or political policy, the Russian government brought its people out of devastation to a level of prosperity unknown to them in Czarist days, and perhaps that level might have equaled that of Western Europe had not Russia been compelled to spend so much of its resources and its manpower upon military reorganization and armament. Though Russia was attacked in 1941 by the strongest, best-trained, best-equipped, and best-led army then in existence, although its defenders were driven across the breadth of European Russia to Stalingrad, its soldiers and people fought with heroic courage and perseverance, beat the invaders back across Russia, back to Berlin, and there put an end to the Second World War. It was American materials that made this historic recovery possible, but it was Russian flesh and blood that made it real.

It was to meet the challenge of communism, as well as to end a critical depression, that Franklin Roosevelt, in the most brilliant statesmanship of the twentieth century, devised the welfare state. President Truman carried this peaceful revolution forward; President Johnson extended it to a scope exceeded only in Great Britain. These Democratic administrations did not enact socialism, but they achieved such a Hegelian synthesis of capitalism and socialism that lifelong socialists like Norman Thomas could feel that they had not lived in vain.

The architects of the welfare state recognized the virtues of capitalism: they perceived the creative stimulus that had been given to invention, enterprise, production, and commerce by the freedom that the laissez-faire governments, after 1789, had

allowed to the acquisitive and competitive instincts of mankind. But they also saw that unchecked liberty permitted the
natural inequality of economic ability to develop an extreme
concentration of wealth, and that most of this wealth was rein-
vested in accelerating production, and that this caused periodic
depressions dangerous to the survival of the system. Of what
use was it that invention, mechanization, and able management multiplied production if the purchasing power of the
people did not grow commensurately?

So an increasing number of capitalists, under the tutelage of
Democratic presidents, learned that they might save—perhaps
enrich—themselves by accepting unions, paying higher wages,
and surrendering more of their profits and salaries to the government. A rising rate of taxation enabled federal and local administrations to spread money in relief, pensions, social
services, education, medical aid, hospital care, and public
works. Some of the concentrated wealth was distributed; the
purchasing power of the people came closer to their ever-
expanding productive capacity; the system worked and spread
abundance, until wealth was again concentrated and necessi-
tated another distribution.

Year by year the government took and disseminated more of
the wealth, managed or controlled more of the economy. Socialism inserted itself into capitalism without destroying it; enterprise, competition, and the pursuit of profit still enjoyed a
stimulating freedom; great fortunes were still made; some of
these were squandered in luxury, revelry, or display—debutante
parties costing $50,000; some, to avoid taxation, were trans-
formed into "foundations" generally helpful to education, science, medicine, and religion; but the greater part of the new
fortunes fell forfeit to the state. The consequent extension of

welfare services by the government, added to automated production and rationalized distribution, reduced poverty to a point lower than any hitherto known to history, though still alarmingly real. Now the rival systems—communism plus dictatorship vs. capitalism plus the welfare state—stand face-to-face in competition for the allegiance of mankind.

My choice between them was not impartial. I was born in the United States; my roots and friends are here; only in a democracy could I have had the opportunities that I have enjoyed for education, freedom to travel, and uncensored authorship. Some of these liberties have been curtailed; for example, I cannot visit Communist China without having my passport withdrawn. But much liberty remains: I can go on strike and join a picket line and I can criticize my government even in fundamental concerns.

Usually internal freedom varies inversely with external danger: the greater the danger the less the freedom. Liberty has diminished in the United States because airplanes and missiles have reduced the power of the oceans to protect us from external attack. As improved communications and transport override frontiers, all major states are caught in a web of perils that erode liberty and make for compulsory order. In the next world war all participating governments will be dictatorships, and all involved economics will be socialist.

Each of the rival systems has drawbacks that their rivalry has helped to reduce. Capitalism still suffers from a periodic imbalance between production and consumption; from dishonesty in advertising, labeling, and trade; from the efforts of large corporations to crush competition; from involuntary unemployment due to the replacement of labor—even of skilled labor—by machinery; and from abnormally swollen fortunes generating resentment in the enclaves of poverty. Communism suffers from the difficulty of substituting governmental prevision of what the consuming public will need or demand for the capitalist way of letting public demand determine what shall be produced and supplied; it suffers from restraints on competition, from inadequate incentives to invention, and from reluctance to appeal to the profit motive in individuals and companies.

Will the cry for personal, political, economic, religious, and intellectual freedom become more insistent in Communist countries while in the West such freedoms will decline as private property yields more and more of its wealth and independence to governmental control? As the Napoleonic Wars hastened the development of industry and capitalism in Western Europe, and as the Civil War had a like effect in the United States, so the two world wars accelerated the transition from individualistic capitalism to state capitalism or government-controlled industry. A hundred signs suggest that the nature of man, the danger and compulsions of conflict, and the growth of communication and trade will eventually bring the competing economies toward basic similarity. (Meanwhile, the diminishing difference can be emphasized by the rival governments to generate the hatreds useful in nationalistic wars.)

The communist and capitalist systems already resemble each other in many basic ways. Each has subordinated its internal economy to the needs of actual or potential war. Each aims at world hegemony, though one disguises its aim in terms of "wars of liberation," the other with the plea that it must serve as the policeman or order in a dangerously chaotic world. Each might be described as a form of capitalism if we define this as a system controlled by the managers of capital: in America some part of the worker's product is kept by private managers to provide private capital for private industry; in communist countries part of the worker's product is kept by public managers (actually by that small fraction of the public called the Communist Party) to provide public capital for public industry. Apparently the American worker—free to organize unions, to strike for higher wages, to radically criticize his masters, to peacefully overthrow a party in power, and to vote himself (through his elected officials) governmental services, pensions, and relief—plays a larger role in determining how much of his product is left, or comes back, to him than does his Communist counterpart. In both systems the men who can manage men manage the men who can manage only things.

Human nature as now constituted seems to favor a system of relatively free enterprise. Every economy, to succeed, must appeal to the acquisitive instinct—the desire for food, goods, and powers, and never in historic times was that impulse so unchecked as under capitalism. The itch for profit may not be overwhelming in the common man, but it is strong in men who are above the average in economic ability; and it is this half of the nation that will sooner or later mold the economy and the laws. We can understand, then, why communism had to make increasing concessions to this instinct. Only slightly less powerful is the urge to sexual union and play; this has obviously more freedom in America and Western Europe than in it does in Communist countries, which struggle to preserve the puritan code associated with their agricultural past. Third among the instincts is the impulse to fight and to compete; this, too, has enjoyed a heady release under capitalism. Unquestionably it shares in improving industrial products; what would Ford and General Motors cars be without their constant rivalry? Despite secret and illegal agreements every product in America is subject to such stimulating rivalry in methods, quality, and price. I wonder whether state control of production in communist countries would allow sufficient competition, among individuals and groups, to realize similar benefits to the consumer? How much of Russia's rapid progress before 1960 was due to free imitation of foreign inventions and processes (themselves the result of free enterprise and competition), and to the importation of foreign machinery and technicians?

The instinct of aggregation favors the Communist system: most men are content, and many are pleased, to follow a leader or join a crowd. We have crowds in America, too, but they are hiding places for lonely individuals, rather than cooperating groups animated by collective actions, pride, and ideals. The reverse of the gregarious instinct—the desire for privacy, for freedom to move about, and to differ from the norm—gets wider play in Western Europe and America than it ever did in Russia, where everyone seemed to live in a confining web of public surveillance, conformity, and control. All in all, the average American (despite the natural protest of the unplaced minority, and of politicians out of office) seems happier, laughs more, ventures more gaily, sins more freely, than his Communist analogue.

CHAPTER NINETEEN

ON ART

I now regret the promise I made, at the outset of this enterprise, to expose myself on every major issue of our time. I wanted to stand up and be counted before seeking sanctuary in the grave. Yet I should have considered that on several basic subjects I would have to speak out of a bottomless well of ignorance and prejudice.

First of all, I am an outsider from art. I have never produced a work of art—never painted a picture since my kindergarten days, never made a statue, even of putty or wax, never built so much as an outhouse. I can lay no claim to understanding the technique or the technical qualities of any art produced in my lifetime (since 1885). For the last fifty years I have been immersed in the study of past forms; I am inclined, consciously or not, to idealize those forms, and to look with suspicion upon those artists who ignore them, or who reject their example and discipline. I may be slightly prejudiced against art itself, for I sense something superficial and unreal in our "cultural explosion," our resolve to be seen at cacophonous concerts that bore us, or in museums that display flaming nonsense as painting and discarded hardware as sculpture. I do not share the view of some flowery esthetes that those who have never heard of Picasso are barbarous plebeians. Nevertheless I proceed.

What are the needs and impulses that make a man spend years of preparation, and then months of labor, to produce a work of art? Presumably because he wishes to express himself, his ideas, and his moods; because he longs for distinction and reward; because he has a keener sense of beauty than most of us; because he aspires to combine the partial beauties and veiled meanings of actual but transitory forms in a vision of clearer significance or more lasting loveliness. Usually he sees more than we see, in fuller intensity or detail; he wishes to remove some of these perceived aspects in order to leave the essence and import of the scene more movingly visible to our eyes and souls. To do this he may deliberately sacrifice beauty, and crowd a wall or canvas with distorted figures, as in El Greco or Modigliani, or with bloated peasants, as in the Brueghels, or with chaotic horrors, as in Hieronymus Bosch.

Philosophers have shown more hesitation in defining beauty than in describing God. Aristotle considered the basic elements of beauty to be symmetry, proportion, and an organic order of parts in a united whole. This conception, like the "Aristotelian unities" in drama, is the classic ideal in literature and art, but it drives Romantic spirits to rebellion and scorn; to them excess is the secret of success, and feeling, not reason, is the source and message of art. Many Japanese artists, tired of symmetry, proportion, and order, found beauty or satisfaction in surprising deviations from regularity of form.

The varying subjective factors in the sense of beauty make an objective definition impossible except in the broadest biological terms. A woman with expansive buttocks may seem beautiful to a Hottentot, or merely appetizing to a starving Turk (on the dietary advantages of steatopygy in a siege, consult Voltaire's *Candide*). One factor, however, is practically universal: most of the higher animals, and all tries of mankind, agree in finding beauty in the opposite sex. The esthetic sense is probably a derivative of sexual desire, display, and selection, and it tends to lose keenness as desire and potency wane. To a normal man, basic beauty lies in the figure, features, and appurtenances of woman. Round forms seem more beautiful than squares because woman is externally a synthesis of curves (hence cubism is a disease); no music is so acceptable to the healthy male as that "gentle voice" which Shakespeare thought "an excellent thing in woman"; and no orchestra can rival a prima donna in her prime.

From this biological origin the sense of beauty spreads to secondary sources in objects consciously or unconsciously reminding us of woman by their smooth surfaces, graceful proportions, bright colors, fragrant odors, or melodious sounds, in clothing, decoration, statuary, painting, or music. Finally the esthetic sense—especially in times of courtship or mating—may overflow to tertiary sources in the softer forms of nature—peaceful landscapes, rounded hills, and babbling streams. By contrast, woman's admiration of strength and security in men may evolve into a sense of sublimity evoked by massive buildings, towering mountains, and majestic or aggressive seas.

To a Romantic soul like mine struggling to be classical (a spirit agitated with feeling but honoring restraint and worshipping form), the most distressing feature of contemporary art is its revolt against beauty. It aims to express an emotion or an attitude rather than to create a pleasing or inspiring form. Just as "modern" or "advanced" women seem resolved to eliminate from their dress all elements of beauty, so a majority of prominent artists since Cezanne turn up their noses at beauty, and a majority of composers since Debussy would rather be found in a brothel than be caught with a deliberate harmony or a melodious line.

The Industrial Revolution may have accustomed us to squares and angles and straight lines, to massive mechanical objects and a wilderness of gleaming lights; and democracy may have leveled Western man's esthetic sense to a common denominator that envies force and is dull to charm. The Rousseauian and individualist revolt against civilization has rejected reason and control, and has slipped into a fanciful cult of barbaric forms; the idolatry of the new has become the worship of the bizarre. "If there is no God," mused Ivan Karamazov, "everything is permitted"; if there are no rules, standards, or models, says the unmoored artist, I can offer anything as art, however formless it may be; I need not study drawing, since shapeless colors suffice to impress the common eye and bilk the millionaires. In art, as in morals, the Bolsheviks have won.

I must make some concessions to this revolution. I admit that change and experiment are essential to development. I can sympathize with the new art's unwillingness to go on painting landscapes, pretty faces, and moneyed heads. I can understand why young artists are sick of hearing about Michelangelo, Raphael, and about Titian, Phidias, Praxiteles, and Donatello; and they have had enough of gods, popes, saints, generals, and statesmen, even of shapely ladies flaunting their petticoats from a swing.

But the rebels carry their revolt against tradition and imitation to a riot of innovation for its own sake; like many tourists they mistake novelty for beauty; they reduce all forms to cubes, or all painting to points, or all reality to "surrealist" dreams, or all sculpture to collages of prosaic hardware or clumsy masses of metal or stone. The most popular of the painters spend their colors upon abstractions that shun every form, follow no logic or theme, communicate no meaning, and dismay a soul that has found order and significance in all the honored art of Europe and Asia.

Abstract art can be noble when it follows form and embodies an aim. Art exists not merely to express but to transmit an emotion, an aspiration, or an idea; otherwise a newsboy proclaiming his wares would be an artist to reckon with. There can be beauty in the abstract art of an Islamic rug or *mihrab*, but in these a line or theme can be followed in its development, thereby pleasing the mind while the color and form please the eye, and usually this art fulfills a purpose, if only to point out a direction or cushion the knees. There can be much beauty in abstract Chinese art, but this has a formal structure and a decorative worth. Any art that has no ruling form is the empty vanity of an undisciplined mind.

I was attracted for a time by Kandinsky's claim that the abstract painter might manipulate colors as a composer marshals tones. Some instances occurred in which this hope seemed to be realized, but, in general, abstract painting in Christendom has lacked the sense of order present in the pure or abstract music of European masters. Much classical music, as in Bach's fugues, Handel's concerti grossi, and Mozart's sonatas, has no meaning, tells no story, offers no idea; however, it transmits a feeling, if only of joy or sorrow, contemplation or piety, strife or peace. A fugue may have no meaning, but it has form, a logical basis, structure, and development, like a missile in its origin, composition, and flight. And the essence of art, as of beauty, lies not in content or elements but in structure and form.

I respond with "enhancement of life" to much "modern" art—by which I mean art since Rodin and Cezanne. Rodin was not the last of the plastic masters; I find grandeur in the sculpture of Ivan Meštrovićá, and I feel the force of Jacob Epstein's colossi; but I shudder at the distortions of Henry Moore. I can see experimental value in Cezanne's distortions, and in the misty vagueness of his line; I can with some effort adjust myself to his slopes and spirals, his cylinders, cones, and cubes. I know that Picasso, when he is not cozening collectors, can excel at will in a dozen varieties of art. I rate highest, among the painters of my time, the Mexican muralists—Rivera, Orozco, and Siqueiros—who announce their ideology in powerful masses of color and form. But when I look at poor Modigliani's hideous figures I sniff the odor of decay. I am not sick enough to like sick art.

I like the architecture of our age, except in houses shoddily flimsy or precariously poised, and churches whose bizarre forms arouse more wonder than worship. (Perhaps their horizontal or wavering platitudes reveal our hopelessness of finding God in the skies.) I admire our skyscrapers; I look upon them not merely as monuments to Mammon but also as science graduating into art, as lusty challenges that men with the courage of their calculations have raised to all the forces of gravity, instability, and dissolution. I amuse my cultured friends by rating the Empire State Building as equal to Chartres Cathedral—though not quite to my ultimate architectural love, Notre Dame de Paris.

When Louis Sullivan proclaimed that "form must follow function," he inaugurated the first creative revolution in architecture since the Renaissance. This brave new style, however, may outmode itself by carrying its functional motto to excess— by reducing everything to straight lines and rectangles, and turning its temples into boxes of steel, stone, and glass imprisoning men in static cubes of rentable space and time. Soon, we may believe, a reaction will restore some curved lines and some tempered ornament, and thereby unite the female principle of beauty with the male principle of strength.

Meanwhile, new arts are being born. Why should we not acknowledge that a handsome automobile is more satisfying to our esthetic sense than most of the sculpture of our age? I pass amazed and delighted by the lovely objects that our department stores offer us in textiles, metal, glass, and wood—should we be ashamed of this happy mingling of the useful with the beautiful? Let us rank among the arts the industrial design that glorifies almost everything that serves us in our daily life. So some old and ailing skills are replaced by new ones, and the sickness of certain contemporary arts may be merely the natural obsolescence of exhausted forms. *Panta rhei*: all things flow, except, perhaps, our categories, prejudices, and tastes.

Art without science is poverty, and science without art is barbarism. Let every science strive to fulfill itself in beauty or wisdom, and let us rejoice when a science becomes an art.

CHAPTER TWENTY

ON SCIENCE

The progress of science has long since outstripped my understanding, and I must take the pronouncements of scientists with the same humility with which I received the dictates of priests and nuns in my youth. I leave it to my grandchildren to break the molecule into its atoms, the atom into its electrons, and these into forces as mystical as the angels that never stood on the point of a pin.

Indeed, a new priesthood is forming above us. Its ordained members speak a language beyond the ken of their worshippers; they censor one another with aromatic praise, and censor one another with professional jealousy; they carry a split atom before them like a consecrated Host; we trust them because they alone have direct access to God—i.e., to mass times the square of the velocity of light. They differ from priests in allowing heresies among the initiated, but let them find an infallible leader, and they would be a church. Already they are as useful and necessary to statesmen as the priests and bishops who surrounded, anointed, and exploited kings.

I honor them, for they hold nothing true unless it has been repeatedly verified by experience. I salute them, for they have worked miracles more marvelous than most of those that once supported religious faith. The apostles, who, we are assured, had the "gift of tongues," would be surprised to learn that a United Nations delegate can address a hundred persons and be heard, a moment later, in half a hundred languages. They would bow their heads before a man who, speaking in Washington, could make himself heard at once through half the world. They would refuse to believe that a man-made machine was sending us pictures taken on the surface of the moon; or that a horse race in Kentucky could be seen as soon, as clearly, and as colorfully in California and Maine as by the spectators on the spot. Verily we live in another age of miracles, and we behold an astonishing new breed of men.

But something of the skepticism that injured my religious faith has overflowed into timid doubts of science. I distrust the astronomers when they calculate the distance of the fixed stars, and the geologists when they tell us the age of the Earth or its strata. I am a bit dubious of the changing pictures by which the physicists represent the inside of the atom; like Pascal, I am oppressed between the ever-elusive infinitesimal and the unattainable, inconceivable infinite. I honor Charles Darwin as the greatest and gentlest revolutionist in modern European history, but I note that biologists have not yet explained how a tiny seed can contain a tree or ordain every branch on the trunk, every leaf on the branch, and every line on the leaf. I think that biology has been misled by applying too widely the notion of mechanism and hesitating to credit living things with inherent, guiding will.

I mourn when I see so much scientific genius dedicated to

the art of massacre, so little to the organization of peace; yet I realize that scientists are not made to rule, since their gift is for handling ideas and facts, not men. Meanwhile I breathe air, and drink water, and eat food polluted by the products of science: by the burning of fuels in factories and cars, by industrial waste poured into our rivers and seas, by dangerous chemicals used in growing or processing foods or disguising their decay. Planes deafen me with their escalating noise, or threaten at any moment to fall upon my head. Sometimes I wonder (as Carlyle did a century ago) would we not be happier if we were living on a medieval farm, accustomed to immemorial poverty, disturbed by nothing beyond our village, and trusting in the wisdom and justice of God.

I puzzle my wits with concocting nostrums for these ills. Many years ago I pled for electric automobiles, and the replacement of filling stations by centers equipped to quickly recharge exhausted batteries. Our chemists, amid all their miracles, have failed to substantially improve the battery in the last thirty years. So now I dream of electric cables laid safely six inches underground in all lanes of our major streets and highways, from which cables every automobile would draw meterable energy by a trolley retractable when changing lanes or directions—in which intervals the car would rely on its own battery. I envision a city clean with electricity produced by nuclear power.

In my Utopia every family, including philosophers, would apply half of its working hours to growing its essential vegetables on a plot of land around or near its house. But since the acquisitive nature of man, and the competitive spirit of states, make this very unlikely, I would beg our educators to give us and our children plentiful instruction in dietetics, in the knowledge of our bodies, and in the care of our health. I would ask our doctors to devote as much time to preventive as to curative procedures, and to put less curative reliance upon drugs and more upon natural cures by diet and physiotherapy. I would like to see health insurance offered to all ages at moderate cost, as in Great Britain; and yet I sympathize with the reluctance of physicians to become governmental employees.

Since 1921 I have inveighed against the absurdities of psychoanalysis. I laughed at Freud's dream theories as soon as I read them. I had had sexual dreams, but never disguised them as cutting a cake. Freud's resort to symbolism in interpreting dreams seemed to me merely the bizarre and unconvincing feat of a diseased imagination. I felt that he had exaggerated sex, and had underrated economic troubles, in generating neuroses; and I had my doubts about "free association" as a means of diagnosis. I had no memory—and had given no reported sign—of having hated my father or of having desired my mother sexually; I don't believe that more than one in a hundred mental disturbances can be traced to the Oedipus complex. Psychotherapy has helped many sufferers, but hardly on the basis of Freudian psychoanalysis. The exaltation and exaggeration of Freudian theories and procedures beyond Freud's own practice and desire has been an incident in the sexual revolution in America.

Every solution bares a new problem. The progress of science has brought new evils with new boons, and its latest victory has given frail minds the power to destroy Western civilization. Periodically we advance pugnaciously to the brink of total war. If such a calamity should come, science might be finished: survivors would flee from their devastated and poisoned cities to the countryside to find or grow food; the age of great cities would end, and a rural Dark Age would begin, as after the triumph of the barbarians over decadent Rome. Religion would revive as the consolation of desperate souls, and men would curse the science that had given them powers beyond their intelligence.

We need more knowledge, and must submit to a heavy stress upon science in education and government, for we are subject to international challenges that force us to keep pace with every technological advance. But we need something more than knowledge; we need the wisdom and character to use our knowledge with foresight and caution, with both resolution and restraint. What is *character*? It is a rational harmony and hierarchy of desires in coordination with capacity. What is *wisdom*? It is an application of experience to present problems, a view of the part in the light of the whole, a perspective of the moment in the vista of years past and years to come.

I do not despair. Man has committed a million blunders evident to our hindsight, but has done great and noble things. He has given us the words of Christ and the *Ethics* of Spinoza; he has built the Parthenon and Notre Dame de Paris; he has adorned the Sistine Chapel and written the *Iliad*, *The Trojan Women*, *The Divine Comedy*, *Hamlet*, *Phèdre*; he has composed the *Messiah* and the lament of Orpheus for Eurydice. Sometimes, like Ashoka and Augustus, he has dared to call off the dogs of war.

Who now will arise to harness our knowledge to wisdom, our science to conscience, our power to humane purposes, our jealous sovereignties to a federated peace? Who will call a halt to hatred, and organize a *Pax Christiana* for our shattered, murderous, suicidal world?

CHAPTER TWENTY-ONE

ON EDUCATION

Herbert Spencer, in a pugnacious little book on education, once challenged the scholastic world with the
question: "What knowledge is of most worth?" He
resented the devotion of youth's years to dead languages, ancient
cultures, and the weary-tramping muses of eighteenth-century
England; such a training, he argued, fitted a man for nothing
but an aristocratic boredom cluttered with classical quotations.
Trained as an engineer, living in the heyday of the Industrial
Revolution, hearing the call of machinery for competent men,
and witnessing with pleasure the rise of the middle class to economic leadership and political influence, Spencer demanded a
schooling that would prepare a man for modern life, that would
ground and equip him realistically for the problems of technology and trade.

He wrote with such clarity and power, and the spirit of the
age was so much with him, that his cause sighted victory before
his death. America, with no strong traditions to impede her,
heard him gladly; Germany, industrializing herself in a genera-

tion with the French indemnity, applied the new theory of education with characteristic thoroughness; Japan, forced into commerce and industry by a world that insisted on arousing her out of her agricultural isolation and content, turned herself to technical education with the immoderate zeal of an anxious convert; and under our eyes Russia moved through a like hyperbola of feverish industrialization in the policy of her government and the training of her youth. Knowledge is power.

Today our educators, who once bravely led the way toward the scientific and technical emphasis in America's schools, are disturbed by the completeness of their victory, and stand in sorrow before their accomplished dream. They do not quite regret their efforts, or retract their aims; they know a modern nation must choose between industry and vassalage, to meet the competition of an industrializing world; these things are not matters of choice, for nations do not live in a vacuum of freedom or peace. But our conscious educators perceive that, after generations of scholastic effort, they are failing to produce either educated men or gentlemen; that the lavish equipment of our schools has not availed to diminish political corruption, sexual irregularity, or violent crime; that certain virtues once prominent in our forbearers seem to have lost standing with a generation skilled beyond precedent in unmoral cleverness; and that the emphasis on science has brought no peace to the soul. These conditions are due rather to economic changes than to pedagogical carelessness; but the educator begins to wonder whether the schools have not surrendered too completely to the charms of the intellect, and offered too mild a resistance to the forces of disorder and decay. When Spencer asked what knowledge is of most worth, he betrayed his secret assumption that education is the transmission of *knowledge*. Is it? What education is of most worth?

That education is of most worth which opens to the body and the soul, to the citizen and the state, the fullest possibilities of their harmonious life. Three basic goods should determine education and define its goals: First, the control of life, through health, character, intelligence, and technology; second, the enjoyment of life, through friendship, nature, literature, and art; and, third, the understanding of life, through history, science, religion, and philosophy. Two processes constitute education and unite in it; in the one, the race transmits to the growing individual its profuse and accumulated heritage of knowledge, techniques, morals, and art; in the other, the individual applies this inheritance to the development of his capacities and the adornment of his life. In proportion as he absorbs this legacy he is transformed from an animal into a man, from a savage into a citizen. Perhaps, if his digestion is good, he is transformed from a simpleton to a sage. Education is the perfecting of life—the enrichment of the individual by the heritage of the race. Let this vital process of transmission and absorption be interrupted for half a century, and civilization would end; our grandchildren would be more primitive than savages.

But these are dull generalities, not unheard before in the halls of education and philosophy. What kind of education, in particular personal, should I wish our children to receive? First of all, and within the limits of nature and circumstance, I should want them to acquire some control over the conditions of their lives. Since the primary condition of life, and the strongest root of happiness, is health, I should like to see them abundantly instructed in the knowledge and care of their bodies.

The body is the visible form and organ of the soul; perhaps, in some wondrous Lamarckian way, it is, through eons of desire and effort, the creation of the soul—form follows function, function follows desire, and desire is the essence of life. Therefore, there is nothing scandalously epicurean in the desire to be physically healthy and clean; cleanliness has been rated next to godliness, and it is difficult to be vicious when one is in perfect health. I should make education in health a required course in every year of schooling from kindergarten to PhD. I should want our children to learn as much about the structure and functioning, the care and healing, of their bodies, as can be taught in an hour a day for fifteen scholastic years. I would have our physicians practice preventive medicine in the classroom by examination and instruction, in the hope that this might reduce the fashionable scissoring of the body in hospitals. I would have our dentists, through unrelenting education and observation in the schools, habituate our children to a diet rough in form and rich in lime, rather than prospect and mine for gold in the decayed teeth of the squirming uninformed. And if the day should come when our dietitians will have at last made up their minds as to what they really know and believe, I should ask them to teach the principles of diet for an hour in every school week for fifteen years, so that our people might make with some corporate intelligence the dietetic changes required by the passage from an outdoor and physical life to a mental and sedentary one. I would teach health and cleanliness first of all, and expect that all things else would be added unto them.

Having sought a sound foundation for the body, I should ask next for the formation of character. I should beg those august boards that exercise the vital function of choosing teachers for our schools to select them—and, so far as possible, to train them—not merely for their technical competence in some blinding specialty, but for the influence which their personalities, their morals, and their manners might have upon the children. Morals and manners cannot easily be taught, but they can be formed; and the presence of a gentleman—that is, a person continuously considerate of all—acts like some mystic magnet upon the growing soul. We have no word in our language to express for the once-weaker sex those qualities which in the male are now connoted by the word *gentleman*; *lady* brings to mind some haughty and bejeweled duchess rather than the simple and understanding kindliness of a woman who has borne children and loved them. If I could have my reactionary way, I would separate the sexes during school hours, though educating them in the same schools; I would have the boys taught by educated gentlemen, and the girls by educated mothers. I am not sure but that some part of the comparative sterility of our educated women is due to their having been trained by women condemned to sterility by economic fears and foolish laws.

Since morality is rooted biologically in the family, I should base moral instruction upon a deliberate exaltation of family life. I would restore the ancient stigma that was attached to celibacy, and would suggest, as delicately as might be, the moral wisdom of marriage at a natural age. The gift of children should be our payment to the race for the heritage of civilization. I would inculcate unremittingly the virtue of filial piety as the foundation stone of morality: A good son makes a good brother, a good father, a good neighbor, and a good citizen. I would extend to the city and the nation the principles of the family; I would ask such persistent moral instruction as would help the individual to see his neighbor as in some degree his brother, and his community as in some degree his family, and to apply to them, in proportion to his development and his strength, those principles of mutual aid which the family plants in the soil as the first necessity of social existence and the highest goal of social organization.

I would solicit from each community some brief formulation of its moral ideals for daily inculcation in the schools, some code of conduct adapted to urban and industrial life, and fitted to simulate individual conscience, commercial honor, and civic pride. I would ask each state to establish and encourage organizations, like the Boy Scouts and the Girl Scouts, that might give to the growing character such vigor and health as could never be instilled by precept alone. Moral excellence, as Aristotle said, is a habit, not an idea. Nor should I hesitate to build up in the child a profound and generous patriotism; for, though I respect and cherish all nations and races that have enriched our racial inheritance, I do not understand how a country can defend itself against attack if its citizens have not learned to love it in some special way as their national hearth and home. I would seek to instill, day after day, a disdain of violence and a respect for law, but I would defend liberty as the essence of personality in a soul or a people; and I would open the schools, at evening, to any public assemblage desired by any significant portion of the community. I would teach not merely the forms and ideals of government but also its worm-eaten reality, so that our children should not look upon corruption as natural and universal, but should never rest until our public life should be as clean and honorable as the best. In short, I should never think it the purpose of education to make scholars, so much as to form human beings.

Perhaps the basic skill that we should ask a teacher to impart to his pupil is the ability to discipline himself; for in this stormy age every individual, like every people, has in the long run only two choices—effective self-government, or practical subjection; somewhere there must be will. In the art of self-discipline intelligence merges with character and becomes the third element in that technique of control, which is the first goal of education. Socrates thought that intelligence was the only real virtue; and if one makes sure to distinguish intelligence from intellect, we may find much virtue and intelligence in his view. *Intellect* is the capacity for acquiring and accumulating ideas; *intelligence* is the ability to use experience—even the experience of others—for the clarification and attainment of one's ends. A man may have a million ideas and yet be a criminal or a fool; it is difficult for an intelligent person to be either.

How shall we train intelligence? This is an esoteric matter, on which I am not competent to speak, and which I prefer to leave to men who can approach it from the background of long experience and patient experiment. Since researches indicate that most learning is by trial and error, we may provisionally conclude that intelligence can hardly be taught in school, but must be acquired through experience and action. The value of letters and literature is that they enable us to acquire more experience than we can gather in the first person; by reading Thucydides, for example, we may learn something of the experiences of Greece; by reading Dostoevsky, we may enter in some measure into the life of Czarist Russia; by reading the *Table Talk* of Napoleon, we catch some glimpse of the world as seen through the eyes of the most realistic of history's Romantic souls. But such vicarious experience is always vague and superficial; first, because only the greatest writers can seize and reveal the essence and meaning of life; and, secondly, because things read seldom enter so deeply into the memory as to affect conduct and character. Science, when it is really science, serves better than literature to train intelligence; for it proceeds by the careful recording and sifting of evidence, the rigid distinction between wishes and facts, and the experimental test of hypothetical conclusions, and it ends in a formulation of some verifiable experience. Through mathematics, physics, and chemistry one may learn to believe according to the evidence, and to weigh all evidence skeptically; if these habits of mind could be formed in all of us, the ability to read or hear would cease to be an impediment to the acquisition of truth, and our raucous age of propaganda might come to an end.

Perhaps the best way to train intelligence in school would be through the manual and domestic arts. Every boy should learn to use the ordinary tools of carpentry and plumbing, and to make minor repairs in the home and on an engine; and every girl should learn the secrets of cookery, household management, and maternal care. There is much pleasure in the simple work of the hands, and, as the old rabbis taught, even the scholar will find that the possession of a trade may save him from selling his conclusions for an income.

As for the girl, it will avail her nothing to know a foreign language, archaeology, and trigonometry, if she cannot manage a home, a husband, and a child; fidelity is nourished through the stomach, and good pies do more for monogamy than all the languages that have ever died. One tongue is enough for any woman, and a good mother is worth a thousand PhDs.

Health, character, and intelligence help us to control ourselves and our lives, and therefore constitute the bases of a free personality, and the primary goals of education. But the same Goethe who held that, in the end, personality is everything, warned us that limits are everywhere. The circle within which we may guide our own lives is a narrow one; surrounding it are the biological, economic, and political compulsions of our state; and beyond these is the spacious realm of accident and incalculable destiny. Education should teach us not only the technique but also the limits of control, and the art of accepting those limits graciously. Everything natural is forgivable.

Within those limits there is so rich a possibility of enjoyment that no lifetime can exhaust it. It should be a second function of education to train us in the art of exploiting these possibilities. First of all, there are human beings around us. They will be gadflies, many of them, and we shall learn to love our privacy as the inner citadel of our content; but many of them will be potential friends, and some of them may be our lovers. I should like my children to be instructed in the give-and-take of human association, in the tolerance that alone can preserve a friendship through growing diversity of interests and views, and in the mutual solitude that perpetually nourishes the fragile plant of love. I should want them to learn something of the origin and development of love, so that they might approach this vital and sometimes destructive experience with a modest measure of understanding. I envision vaguely some leisurely course in human relations, running for perhaps an hour a week through fifteen years, and culminating in a study of what the wisest of men and women, the most delicate of scientists and the most forgiving of philosophers, have said about marriage.

Next to human beings around us, the greatest source of our pleasures and pains will be Nature herself. I should like our children to recognize the terror as well as the beauty in Nature, and to accept the naturalness of struggle, suffering, danger, and death; but I should wish them to be sensitive to all those aspects of earth and sky that can move the soul with loveliness or sublimity. In my youth I rejected astronomy, botany, and ornithology as dismal catalogues of names; I thought I should be able to enjoy flowers, birds, and stars as well without as with a knowledge of their nature, their relationships, and their names. I suspect now that I was wrong, and that our children are wrong today; for they, too, with an obstinacy that I recognize as my own, refuse to have anything to do with these effeminate sciences. But I wish I had learned better to distinguish a planet from a star, a sparrow from an eagle, and a chrysanthemum from a rose; I think that if I knew these lustrous forms more intimately and individually, and could call them by their first names, I should enjoy them more, if only with the half-conscious pleasure that one derives from the presence of familiar things.

Certainly I should like our children to be at home with Nature's infinite variety; to love not merely her verdure and blossoming, but her mystic mists and mellow decay; to enjoy the ocean like Byron, and the sun like Turner, and the rain like Whistler, and the nightingale like Keats. I think I should have a course in Nature running pleasantly through my children's years, and ranging from a recognition of the Pleiades to the art of making a garden grow. I would have them explore the Wissahickon, and camp in the Adirondacks, and paddle their own canoes up or down a hundred streams with melodious names such as once lured the poets of England to dream of a Utopia on the Susquehanna's shores. I would be happy to see them enjoying the spectacle of sports, but happier to see them sharing in them. I would give academic credit for swimming, baseball, football, basketball, and those other lusty games that require and develop more intelligence and character than all the conjugations of Greece and Rome.

I do not think I should bother them with foreign languages at all. I studied Latin and Greek for seven years, taught them for four, and talked one of them, on and off, for two; I found some moments of pleasure in them, but many hours of unnatural syntactic pain; they rarely helped me to enjoy or understand the geniuses of the classical world; and today, when I wish to renew acquaintance with Homer or Euripides, Virgil or Lucretius, I turn not to the originals, which are associated in my memory with an aimless drudgery, but to such translations as Chapman or Gilbert Murray made, or William Morris and William Ellery Leonard. Even the modern foreign languages are hardly fit for the classroom; one never learns them from books, however patiently suffered and perused; if you wish to learn French, go live with the French, and throw the grammars to the grammarians, who are the only ones that have ever profited from them. It is said that a knowledge of Latin helps one to write English well, and perhaps it is so, though nothing is so deadly as the English of Latinists; for my own part, I would rather spend my tutelage in English with Bacon and Milton, Addison and Burke, Gibbon and Macaulay and Newman than with a tongue idiomatically alien to my own. Philologists should be encouraged to learn and preserve Latin and Greek for the purposes of scholarship and history, but there is no more reason for making a dead language compulsory than for compelling the student to learn an obsolete trade. There is but one decent thing for most of us to do with a dead language, and that is to bury it.

But after interring the languages of Greece and Rome I would give to their living literatures most of the time once spent on the dry bones of their grammars and lexicons. I never knew how rich the Greek genius was until I stopped reading Greek. The dramas of Euripides had been a dreary task in the original; the translations of Gilbert Murray, though overfree, were a revelation; let the reader give an hour to *The Trojan Women* and share my exaltation. I would spare my pupils Greek, but not Greece; I would spur them on to study that exuberant civilization as some standard by which to measure and brighten their own. I would lure them into the fascinating gossip of Herodotus, and the vivid biographies of Plutarch; they would take their time and pleasure leisurely with Homer, and sport awhile with Sappho and Anacreon; they would watch Solon legislating for Athens, Pericles governing the mob, Demosthenes denouncing demagogues, and Phidias carving the pediments of the Parthenon. Then we should turn and study Caesar—not the cold and repetitious prose of the *Gallic Wars*, but Caesar himself, in all his living personality and tragedy; we should abandon ourselves to Virgil's *Aeneid* as a very pleasant tale; we should meet the early emperors in Arthur Murphy's *Tacitus*; we should drown ourselves in the ocean of Gibbon's prose, and pass with him into the somber magic, the scholastic subtlety, and the rural jollity of the Middle Ages, and the pious butchery, the sensuous poetry, and architectural embroidery of Islam.

Literature, then, would open for us a third portal to the enjoyment of life. We would read George Moore's *Heloise and Abelard*, and the profoundly beautiful letters ascribed to Heloise; we would wander through Dante's delectable *Inferno* with Norton or Cary; and we would pass over to Persia and lose ourselves in the luscious quatrains of FitzGerald's *Omar Khayyám*. We would browse at our pleasure in Symonds's exhilarating volumes on the Renaissance; we would listen to Machiavelli telling Cesare Borgia how to be a successfully Machiavellian prince; we would let Cellini recount his incredible adventures to us, and would have Vasari play Plutarch to Leonardo, Michelangelo, and Raphael. We would smile with Montaigne, and laugh with Rabelais; we would smash windmills with Don Quixote, and tear our hearts out with Shakespeare; we would sharpen our wits with Bacon's *Essays*, and our tongues with the divine monkey of Ferney; we would read some of Milton's poetry, and more of his royal prose; we would hear Rousseau's confession, and let the mighty Johnson "sir" us to his heart's content. We would be willingly swallowed up in the Romantic Movement of European poetry; we would fret and fume with Byron, laugh and cry with Heine, hope and mourn with Shelley, and suffer the world's beauty and tragedy with Keats; we would explore the sewers of Paris with Jean Valjean, and the horrors of Carthage's wars with the lovely Salammbô. We would enter the crowded world of Balzac, and watch the sadistic Flaubert tear his heroes and heroines to pieces; we would share the vicissitudes of Becky Sharp, David Copperfield, and the Pickwick Club; we would parse Browning and sing Tennyson. Then we would come home and let Whitman chant his healthy song for us; we would whittle pencils at Walden Pond with Thoreau, and rock ourselves to sleep with the musical wisdom of Emerson; we would read the letters and speeches of Lincoln slowly, and let his profound and understanding spirit brood over us until we knew the worst and best of America.

Is this a heavy program for the helpless boys and girls of our schools and colleges? But still another avenue of education for enjoyment must be traveled by them—and that the most difficult of all. I should not bother them with art beyond their liking, for beauty need not be wasted on those who have no eyes or ears for it; but if they cared at all for painting or sculpture, architecture or music, I would put every opportunity in their way. I would ask them to hear every year for four years both the *Emperor Concerto* and *St. Matthew's Passion*, until through repetition these compositions might reach beneath their ears and lift them above rubbish forever. I would take the most willing ones to the great museums and bid them sit quietly for a while before Raphael's *Julius II*, or Rembrandt's rabbis or Rembrandts; I would, if I could, take them all the way to England to worship the mother goddess Demeter or the goddesses of Phidias in the British Museum; I would let them spend a week at Chartres or Rheims, a week in Greece, a month in Italy, and a day at Granada, so that they might know that size is not development, so that there might begin to burn in them that flame of the love of perfection which builds amid the ocean of life, upon the volcano of civilization, the fragile citadel of art.

When my children enter college I trust that education will open to them many paths toward the understanding of life. "May my son study history," said Napoleon at St. Helena, "for it is the only true philosophy, and the only true psychology." Psychology is largely a theory of human behavior, philosophy is too often an ideal of human behavior, and history is occasionally a record of human behavior. We cannot trust all the historians, for sometimes, like Akbar's, they were engaged by their heroes and gave them all the virtues and the victories. But no man is educated, or fit for statesmanship, who cannot see his time in the perspective of the past. Every lad and lass should begin, in high school, an orderly recapitulation of the pageant of history; not, as we used to do, with Greece and Rome, which were the old age of the ancient world, but with Mesopotamia and Egypt and Crete, from which civilization flowed over into Greece and Rome, and through them to Northern Europe and ourselves.

In the second year of high school they would study the classical cultures with some such perfect textbook as Breasted's *Ancient Times*, and should steal at least a glance at Buddha's India and the China of Confucius; in the third year they would study the Middle Ages and the Renaissance, the heyday of Islam in Cordova and Baghdad, the great ages of India under the Guptas and the Moguls, and the flowering of Chinese poetry and art in the Tang Dynasty.

In the first year of college they would begin modern history and try to absorb some of the wealth of European culture, from Luther and Leo X to the French Revolution; in their second college year they would follow the vicissitudes of revolution and democracy from 1789 to the Second World War; and in the third they would review, with better understanding than in their grammar grades, the history of America from the Mayas and the Incas to their own generation. It would be but an introduction to history; the college mind could hardly cope with the master works of Thucydides and Grote, Mommsen and Gibbon, Voltaire and Guizot, Ranke and Michelet, Macaulay and Carlyle, Charles and Mary Beard. But it would give the young student such a perspective of human affairs from the first pyramid to the last election as might fit him to think and move more intelligently among the issues of his time.

A second door to the understanding of life would be through science, understood now not as a tool of conquest but as a description of the external world. Here would belong all the nebulous hypotheses of astronomic origins and development; all the brave guesses of geology as to the history of the Earth; all the theories of the origin and development of life. Better than these theories would be a firsthand study of plant and animal life in the fields and the streams and the woods; perhaps a little dissection of dead life in the laboratory; above all, a realistic understanding of life as a matter of hunger and love, inequality and insecurity, competition and cooperation, elimination and selection, destruction and creation, bloodshed and tenderness, peace and war.

A pleasanter path to understanding is philosophy. In Plato's view, this "dear delight" should not be permitted to youth for, said the master, youngsters debate the problems of human life with no desire for truth but only a blind hunger for victory; they tear and bite at one another with arguments, and the truth, in the end, lies torn and tattered at their feet. Perhaps the college student should content himself, in his final year, with a course in the history of philosophy; a course that should center around the great personalities, and make wisdom human for the adolescent mind. In such a course Plato's *Republic* could be a sufficient text; let the student realize how old our current problems are, and for how many centuries the nature of men has played havoc with the ideals of philosophers and saints. Then, while he winds his way slowly through the still fresh meadows of Plato's thought, let our college boy or girl rub elbows for a while with Aristotle, Zeno, and Epicurus, with Lucretius, Epictetus, and Marcus Aurelius, with Aquinas and Occam, Descartes and Spinoza, Bacon and Hobbes, Kant and Schopenhauer, Comte and Spencer, Nietzsche and Spengler. If these are too difficult for him, let the student seek wisdom from those supreme writers who transformed philosophy into drama, fiction, and poetry; let him strike up acquaintance with Sophocles and Euripides and Aristophanes, Dante and Shakespeare and Goethe, Hardy and Dostoevsky and Tolstoy. It is good if he even merely learns the names of the philosophers, and derives from them a firm conviction that there is such a thing as philosophy; in later years, if life leaves him leisure for speculation, he may return to these men, grapple with them in a fierce resolve to master them, and work his way through the unsettlement of every belief to some plateau of clearer insight, of more modest aspiration and gentler doubt. Perhaps in that unimpeded air he will see all philosophies as but one groping, all faiths as but a single hope; it will not be in his heart to fight any of them any longer, or to refuse the fellowship of his mind to any honest creed; a great sympathy for all the dreams of men, a loving understanding of all their harassed ways, will widen and deepen him, and he will know the peace and simplicity, the tolerance and catholicity, of the sage.

It is evident that education cannot be completed in school or college or university; these offer us only the tools and maps for those farther-ranging studies that lead to the control, the enjoyment, and the understanding of life. I have said nothing of travel, which, if it is too varied and hurried, makes the mind more superficial and confirms it in its prejudices, but which, if it implies a receptive residence in foreign scenes, may reveal to the soul some image of that total perspective which is the ever-alluring mirage of philosophy. I have said nothing of the technical disciplines that aim to prepare the student for his avocation, for I do not believe that these should begin during his college years. I would shorten both the high school and the college course to three years each; I would give the first fifteen years of education to establishing the physical, moral, and cultural background of life, and would leave specific technical training to postgraduate schools. It is my hope that within my lifetime half the youth of America will pass through college, and that half of these will pass through such graduate technical schools. As invention proceeds, we shall need an ever-greater supply of trained technicians and an ever-smaller supply of arms and legs. There is no reason why invention should not reduce nearly all menial labor to machinery in the not-too-distant future, and leave man essentially an intellectual factor in production. The proletariat, instead of dictating, will disappear.

I believe that European education is more thorough in its methods and finer in its product than ours; partly through a longer and more stable tradition that intercepts fads and frills at their birth; partly through a wise concentration of scholastic time upon a smaller variety of subjects; partly through the separation of the sexes and the avoidance of sexual distraction in school; and partly through the severer demands made upon the student both in the quantity of work required and in the strictness of discipline maintained. We must not expect to rival the best European colleges in our generation, for time is the chief ingredient of every institution; but we should send the ablest of our normal-school graduates to study the educational methods of England, Germany, and France, in the hope that we may add their excellences to ours, and go beyond them in the end.

Despite our difficulties and our sufferings in these hesitating years, we are well placed in America for building better than men have ever built before. We have in our soil a physical legacy of unparalleled resources, and in our population a stock still abounding in vitality, inventiveness, and skill. We have in our traditions, our libraries, and our schools a cultural accumulation from many continents and ages that is so full in scope and content that no one mind could compass a thousandth of its wealth. It is the function and high destiny of education to pour this civilizing heritage into this vigorous stock, that the gifts of the earth may be more intelligently exploited than before, that our prosperity may be more widely distributed, and that our riches may flower into finer manners and morals, profounder literature and saner art. I do not doubt that on this broadest basis of educational opportunity and material possibilities ever known, we shall build a society and a civilization comparable with the best, and capable of adding some measure of wisdom and beauty to the inheritance of mankind.

CHAPTER TWENTY-TWO

ON THE INSIGHTS OF HISTORY

Let us now see what that vast laboratory of human history has to say about the issues I have so imperfectly touched upon. To begin, the patterns of our behavior down through the centuries can only be seen by looking at history in the large, rather than in isolated segments. I'll admit that viewing history this way is not popular with many academics and specialists. Still we proceed.

"History," said Henry Ford, "is bunk." As one who has written history for almost sixty years, and studied it for almost eighty, I should largely agree with the great engineer who put half the world on wheels. History as it is typically studied in schools—history as a dreary succession of dates and kings, of politics and wars, of the rise and fall of states—this kind of history is verily a weariness of the flesh, stale and flat and unprofitable. No wonder so few students in school are drawn to it; no wonder so few of us learn any lessons from the past.

But there is another way in which to view history; history as man's rise from savagery to civilization—history as the record of the lasting contributions made to man's knowledge, wisdom, arts, morals, manners, skills—history as a laboratory rich in a hundred thousand experiments in economics, religion, literature, science, and government—history as our roots and our illumination, as the road by which we came and the only light that can clarify the present and guide us into the future—that kind of history is not "bunk"; it is, as Napoleon said on St. Helena, "the only true philosophy and the only true psychology." Other studies may tell us how we *might* behave, or how we *should* behave; history tells us how we *have* behaved for six thousand years. One who knows that record is in large measure protected in advance against the delusions and disillusionments of his times. He has learned the limitations of human nature, and bears with equanimity the faults of his neighbors and the imperfections of states. He shares hopefully in the reforming enterprises of his age and people; but his heart does not break, nor his faith in life fade out, when he perceives how modest are the results, and how persistently man remains what he has been for sixty centuries, perhaps for a thousand generations.

It is a mistake to think that the past is dead. Nothing that has ever happened is quite without influence at this moment. The present is merely the past rolled up and concentrated in this second of time. You, too, are your past; often your face is your autobiography; you are what you are because of what you have been; because of your heredity stretching back into forgotten generations; because of every element of environment that has affected you, every man or woman that has met you, every book that you have read, every experience that you have had; all these are accumulated in your memory, your body, your character, your soul. And so it is with a city, a country, a race; it is its past, and cannot be understood without it. It is the present, not the past, that dies; this present moment, to which we give so much attention, is forever flitting from our eyes and fingers into that pedestal and matrix of our lives which we call the past. It is only the past that lives.

Therefore I feel that we of this generation give too much time to news about the transient present, too little to the living past. We are choked with news, and starved of history. We know a thousand items about the day or yesterday, we learn the events and troubles and heartbreaks of a hundred peoples, the policies and pretensions of a dozen capitals, the victories and defeats of causes, armies, and athletic teams—but how, without history, can we understand these events, discriminate their significance, sift out the large from the small, see the basic currents underlying surface movements and changes, and foresee the result sufficiently to guard against fatal error or the souring of unreasonable hopes?

"History," said Lord Bolingbroke, quoting Thucydides, "is philosophy teaching by examples." And so it is. It is a vast laboratory, using the world for its workshop, man for its material, and records for its experience. A wise man can learn from other men's experience; a fool cannot learn even from his own. History is other men's experience, in countless number through many centuries. By adding some particles of that moving picture to our vision we may multiply our lives and double our understanding. I propose now to look at man in the successive stages of life and the major phases of our activity, and to ask if history has any light to shed upon the issues of our time.

OUR NATURE

History sees the newborn child as the product of millions of years, during most of which he was a hunter fighting for his food and his life against beasts stronger than himself except for his use of weapons and tools. Those years formed the basic nature of our species: acquisitiveness, greed, competition, and pugnacity tending to violence. Man, to become civilized, must be subjected to a system of national law possessing superior force, just as states, to be civilized, must be subjected to a system of international law possessing superior force. So we must relinquish the childish dreams of unfettered liberty that inspired many of us in our youth, and that still enthrall some college students in America and abroad. And though we acknowledge that poverty is a spur to crime, we perceive that the root of crime, in all classes, nations, and ages, is the basically lawless nature of man, formed by a million years of hunting, fighting, killing, and greed.

History finds that human nature is essentially the same in ancient and in modern civilizations, in the poor as in the rich, in radicals as in conservatives, in underprivileged peoples as in affluent states. If anything is clear in the experience of mankind it is that successful revolutionists soon behave like the men they have overthrown: Robespierre imitates the Bourbons, and Stalin imitates the czars. Hence history smiles at revolutions as understandable reactions but unprofitable and transient; they may give vent to just resentment, but they produce only surface change; under the new names and phrases the old realities survive.

POPULATION

The child is an immediate problem as well as a potential delight, for he embodies both a threat of quantity and a threat to
quality. He cries out to be fed, and the food supply—taking the
earth as a whole—has seldom kept up with the birthrate. In
some highly exceptional periods the deaths have exceeded the
births, as during the bubonic plague of the fourteenth century,
or the Thirty Years' War of the seventeenth. But normally it is
harder to produce food than to beget children; so in nearly all
ages the growth of population has outrun the production of
food, and the balance between births and deaths has been restored by the ruthless Malthusian trinity of famine, pestilence,
and war.

The opening of new lands, and the improvement of agricultural methods and machinery in the last hundred years, enabled
Western Europe and North America to escape famine despite a
rapid population growth; and the recent spread of better seeds
and artificial fertilizer has allowed China and India to feed their
proliferating millions. But how long can we defer the explosive
confrontation between the limited productivity of arable soil
and the uncontrolled reproductive ecstasy of men? Already the
cry of the hungry threatens the stability of a world in which
some nations and classes are near starvation and others are dete-
riorating into luxury and obesity. I hail it as a sign of progress
that the United States is exporting contraceptives to India, and,
in America, offering them to all who legitimately need them.

Again, the child embodies a threat to quality, for he may be
the careless product of parents unfit to bear or rear offspring.
Some studies have suggested that superior mental ability can be
transmitted from parent to child. Even if this is uncertain, and

though superior intelligence may come rather from an incalculable gamble of the genes and from environmental opportunity and stimulus, we must face the fact that a reckless fertility can cancel much of the work of the educator in each generation. So we advance in literacy but not visibly in intelligence; yet democracy must depend upon public intelligence.

It is usual to ascribe the fall of the Western Roman Empire to barbarian invasion from without; could it have been due in part to barbarian multiplication within? Sometimes I think that we have reached a similar peril in the United States: the older American stocks still dominate in industrial and political leadership and skill but many families breed carelessly, live riotously, ignore the laws, and transform America's literature, art, music, and dance into primitive crudities while many of their spokesmen proclaim and pray for the collapse of the American government. Civilization is a fragile bungalow precariously poised on a live volcano of barbarism.

THE FAMILY

As mentioned earlier, until the nineteenth century the family was the economic as well as the biological and moral unit of society. The father taught and managed his sons in work on the farm; the mother taught and managed her daughters in the hundred arts of the home; and this dependence and tutelage of the children formed the economic basis of parental authority. The Industrial Revolution, by drawing sons and daughters into independent employment, deprived parental authority of its economic base. So the family, which for thousands of years served as the fount and bastion of disciplined character and social order, lost its economic functions and its moral force. The individual, freed from the family, idolized liberty and did not learn till too late that liberty is a child of order and may be the mother of chaos. He looked down upon his parents as belonging to an ignorant past, and proudly announced an unbridgeable gap between the generations.

THE SCHOOL

The school tried to take over from the disintegrating family the task of disciplining the young and passing on to them the civilizing heritage and experience of the past. But the growth of knowledge compelled the teacher to specialize; he became an intellectual fragment transmitting intellectual fragments to youths bewildered and unmoored; in the United States and France education became almost wholly a furnishing of the intellect; the formation of character was turned back by the teacher to the family and the Church. But as these were losing their power, the student grew daily in sharpness of intellect and looseness of character. For the intellect is a constitutional individualist; it thinks of the self first, and only in its mature development does it consider the group.

There have been student rebellions many times in history, and in some cases, as in thirteenth-century Bologna, the students controlled the selection, payment, and dismissal of some professors; this ended when Bologna became part of the Papal States and the Church appointed the faculty. Usually student riots were against the townsmen rather than against the teachers or the curriculum. Today they are against the relation, or lack of relation, between the curriculum and the world.

The angry student resents courses that do not prepare him for successful functioning in a technological society, or that ignore the role of ethnic minorities in our history. He resents the absorption of teachers in private research and the domination of physical, biological, and chemical research by the needs of the army for ever more effective means of inflicting or avoiding wholesale death. The student began by admiring the marvels of science; he ends by distrusting science as mechanizing life and industry, and as selling itself to the military industrial complex that dominates both the individual and the state.

An alarming number of our children turn their backs upon the struggle and drop out not only from education but also from civilization, repudiating its graces and amenities. They reject the past as irrelevant in a hectically changing world and repudiate the wisdom of their elders as geared to a vanished scene. Finally they take to narcotics to escape the responsibilities of life; and we who rightly reprove them are ourselves bewildered and groping, and paralyzed with fear of what our unmoored children may do or become.

RELIGION

Once the task of civilizing the young was assumed by religion and its rituals; through twenty-five centuries the synagogue and the Church inculcated morality by the Ten Commandments, and strengthened them by ascribing to them a divine origin and an ever-present sanctioning of reward or punishment. But the Church and the synagogue have lost much of their efficacy as sources of social order because, in our major cities, half the adult population has discarded supernatural beliefs.

We enter an age like the Hellenistic in Greece and the Imperial in Rome, when the classical religions had passed from creeds and rites encouraging patriotism and morality into a mythology providing poets with pretty legends and Zeus with many mistresses. Caesar laughed when filling his required role as supreme pontiff, and Ovid wrote beautifully about the gods but lasciviously about love. Social chaos so threatened the ancient order that the emperor Constantine, in AD 380, adopted Christianity as the state religion, partly because it gave promise of restoring morality. From that time till Darwin religion was relied upon by the state to give morals to youth, order to society, and hope to the oppressed. Where now is the religion or the faith that will once again inspire us and give a soul to our civilization?

MORALITY

From these changes in the economics and theology of the last one hundred years has come the moral dissolution of our time. The new freedom spread and released sexual behavior from old restraints. Psychology has seemed to condemn every inhibition, and to justify every desire. Literature, in the hands of some of its most skilled practitioners, has become a paramour of pornography.[1] The dissemination of wealth has opened a hundred doors that used to be called sin. Dishonesty among adults—in business, advertising, politics, the practice and administration of the law—weakens the preachments of the old. Inventions gave new tools to the criminal; the automobile made easier his escape, court decisions made his conviction more difficult; and prison associations made murderers out of petty thieves.

Has history known other periods of like moral laxity? Yes—usually in ages of mercantile wealth, urban concentration, and religious decline. You will recall Sophist Hellenistic Greece, Imperial Rome, Renaissance Italy, Elizabethan England, and the Stuart Restoration. Hear Plato, writing about 390 BC, and using Socrates for his mouthpiece:

> *Socrates*: In such a state the anarchy grows and finds a way into private houses, and ends by getting among the animals and infecting them. . . . The father gets accustomed to descend to the level of his sons . . . and the son to be on a level with his father, having no fear of his parents, and no shame. . . . The master fears and flatters his scholars, and the scholars despise their masters and tutors. . . . Young and old are alike, and the young man is on a level with the old, and is ready to compete with him in word or deed; and old men . . . imitate the young. Nor must I forget to tell of the liberty and equality of the two sexes in relation to each other. . . . Truly, the horses and asses come to have a way of marching along with all the rights and dignities of free men . . . all things are just ready to burst with liberty. . . .
>
> *Adeimantus*: But what is the next step?
>
> *Socrates*: The excessive increase of anything often causes a reaction in the opposite direction. . . . The excess of liberty, whether in states or individuals, seems only to pass into slavery . . . and the most aggravated form of tyranny arises out of the most extreme form of liberty.[2]

Following the suggestion of Plato, we may expect to find pagan and puritan periods following in mutual reaction in history. The Hellenistic and Roman relaxation was succeeded by the strict morality of the spreading Christian communities, which continued till the thirteenth century. Then Italy, having developed a rich commerce and collecting religious revenues from all Western Christendom, provided the wealth that financed the Renaissance; with that wealth, and those foreign contacts and influences, came the loosened faith of the humanists, and the loosened morals of princes, peoples, and popes.

The Protestant Reformation was in one sense a puritan reaction of the poorer North against an opulent and re-paganized Italy; not so much in the lusty Luther, as in the stern Calvin and obsessed Knox. But in England the spread of commerce under Elizabeth I and James II brought a growth of luxury and a relaxing of morals that combined to release and promote an outburst of romantic poetry, high drama, and noble prose.

The excesses of that pagan release brought in the ascendancy of the Puritans, who raised Cromwell to power and put Charles I to death. The Puritan regime covered England with such gloom, hypocrisy, and censorship that she rejoiced when Charles II brought a new age of moral laxity and literary license. The Restoration ended when the Dutch stadtholder was called in and displaced the last of the Stuart kings. Queen Anne, in 1702, began that Augustan Age which brought morality back in fashion, and classical restraint back to style. This semi-Puritan compromise was interrupted by the revolutionary ardor and romantic flair of Wordsworth's youth, Shelley's poetry, and Byron's death but it was resumed under Queen Victoria.

While Victoria brooded over her princes and paupers the Industrial Revolution changed and darkened the face of England; English commerce covered the seas and British fleets made the world safe for aristocracy. Women were emancipated from the home for labor in the shops, and sex was freed from parentage; science flourished, religion declined, wealth liberated desire, and that new age of paganism began in which we live today.

According to this historical alternation of paganism and puritanism, we should expect our present moral laxity to be followed by some return to moral restraint under old or new forms of belief, authority, and censorship. Every age reacts against its predecessor. If a Third World War should come, shattering our cities, and driving the survivors back to agriculture, the age of science may end, and religion may return with its consolatory myths and its moral discipline, and parental authority may be restored.

WORK

Sooner or later the growing individual, unless he drops out from the game of life, leaves the irresponsibilities of freedom for the demand and discipline of the job. Soon he begins to feel the complexity of capitalism: its varied, far-reaching roots in enterprise, materials, fuels, science, money, and men; its obligation to meet ever-new forms of competition and inventions, its grasping tentacles of domestic marketing and foreign trade; its ever-changing relations to public demand, organized labor, and state and federal law. A moment of modesty may come over him as he is confronted by his subtle product of greed and genius, trial and error, through the centuries. He may wonder if his rebellious generation can tear to pieces this vast mechanism of mind and matter, capital and skill, and put it together again nearer to his dream.

How does this American capitalism compare with other

economic systems in history? In productivity, of course, it has no equal, and no precedent. Never before has an economic system poured forth so great and varied an abundance of goods and services, tools and labor-saving devices, books and journals, comforts and amusements—a theater, a music hall, a marketplace in almost every home. Never before has woman been so free, so embellished, or so learned. Never before has labor had such short hours or long leisure, such influence in government, such power of determining its own rewards. Never before has so large a proportion of the people been raised to so high a standard of living.

Is the worker dulled by the monotony of his task? Not so much as in the twelve-hour day of early capitalism; probably no more than the shoemaker over his last, the tailor over his needle, the shepherd with his flock, the plowman, tiller, and gleaner in the field.

Are the American people less happy than their ancestors? I think not. See them, even the poor, in their games or on the bleachers, or driving off on a holiday in their Cadillacs or Fords, making all of America their playground and their theater. Are they more materialistic than in preindustrial days? In the Middle Ages few individuals had any hope of rising out of the class (even little hope of leaving the locality) in which they had been born; so they may have been less agitated by that itch for advancement which stimulates most Americans today. But we must not populate medieval Europe with replicas of John Ruskin and William Morris; probably the Gothic architects and sculptors worked to support their families, and Raphael's Madonnas fed him as well as their bambini. Even the hope of heaven may have been a long-term investment of pence and penance for a guaranteed perennial return.

Has history displayed any effective substitute for the profit motive as a spur to work, invention, or production? Experiments have been made to get things done for nonfinancial rewards—prizes, medals, ribbons, titles, etc.; they have succeeded for a time with select individuals but never long with the labor force of a community. Soviet Russia, in its early ardor, tried to replace the profit motive with appeals to communistic devotion, but it soon discovered that, as Aristotle had warned, "when everybody owns everything nobody takes care of anything." So the Soviets returned to unequal pay for unequally valuable or skillful work. There is now in Russia as great a gap in remuneration between simple and complex work as in American industry.

But our exciting capitalism is showing dangerous defects. It is poisoning our air, our waters, perhaps even our food. It has been killing the fish in our streams and seas and the birds in the sky. It has been using at a reckless rate the mineral resources of our soil. Above all, it seems by its very nature to stimulate repeated concentrations of wealth, leading to contractions of purchasing power and to depressions. Of course, wealth has always tended to flow uphill and seek a crest—whether in martial conquerors, hereditary monarchs, ecclesiastical potentates, or feudal lords; you cannot make men equal by passing laws.

Repeatedly, in history, this natural concentration of wealth has led to a pathological, almost cancerous, condition. Sometimes it has led to ruinous surgery by revolution, as in Rome from the Gracchi to Caesar, or in France from Mirabeau to Napoleon. Sometimes statesmanship has devised a less sanguinary treatment, as by the remedial legislation of Solon in 594 BC or Franklin Roosevelt in 1933; then the tumor was reduced by the painful but bloodless taxation of swollen wealth and its partial redistribution through made-work and the welfare state.

But after each redistribution—violent or peaceful—the concentration begins anew: the clever individual gets the best inventions, the best loans, the best jobs, the best land, and the best homes; in time the inequality of possessions is as before. So, economic history, in this aspect, is the slow heartbeat of the social organism, a vast diastole and systole of concentrating wealth and explosive revolution.

Naturally, therefore, the cry for revolution rises again in the Americas, France, and Italy; not only as echoes of Russia and China, but as the protest of bitter poverty living side by side with proud wealth (as in First and Fifth Avenues in New York), and as the plaint of college students eager to organize the weak to overthrow the strong.

Revolt, of course, is an inborn right of youth; it is a mark of the ego become conscious of itself and demanding a place in the world. My own generation shouted rebellious slogans—the right of labor to organize, of women to vote, of workers to be better paid, of schools and universities to be open to all, of speech and press to be free. I am encouraged when I think how many of these objectives have been attained.

But the current revolt among the young goes deeper. They do not complain that they have not become millionaires; many of them profess to scorn material possessions. (I am reminded of the Lollards, wandering preachers of fourteenth-century England, or of the Anabaptists of sixteenth-century Germany, or of the wandering scholars of the late Middle Ages, who composed and sang songs of freedom and rebellion, even of free love.) Their challenge is to our ruthless competition, our greed for possessing wealth and power, our barbaric wars for the raw materials of the earth, the refusal of our governments to obey the moral code that it preaches to its citizens.

Just as those frockless preachers helped to prepare the Reformation, so it may be that our present rebels will open the way to a constructive reshaping of our ideals in the decades to come. I leave aside the aimless and disheveled minority that seem to have no higher purpose than to note what their elders do and then do the opposite in order to flaunt their egos in the face of the world. These are the lost. However, when our young students talk of revolution I wonder have they compared their light-armed infantry with the heavy weaponry of a modern state? And when we ask how, if they won, they could reorganize industry and government before chaos universalized destitution, they have no answers but faith, hope, and love ending in dictatorship.

Such a dénouement of democracy would not be new to history. Almost four centuries before Christ, Plato, in *The Republic*, reduced the transit of governments to a regular and repetitious cycle: from chaos to dictatorship and monarchy, from monarchy to aristocracy, from aristocracy to democracy, from democracy to chaos, from chaos to dictatorship . . .

I know of no way of avoiding the toboggan of democracy into revolutionary chaos and authoritarian dictatorship except through the welfare state checked by birth control. Though there are many sluggards among the poor, and discouraging abuses in the administration of relief, we must recognize that the majority of the poor are victims of racial discrimination and environmental handicaps. We must tax ourselves to provide adequate education, and a minimum of food, clothing, contraceptives, and shelter for all, as a far less costly procedure than social and political disorder through minority violence and authoritarian force, crushing between them not only democracy but perhaps civilization itself.

WAR

The solution to domestic problems is hampered by the spiral-
ing cost of protecting ourselves from alien interference with our
internal liberty or our access to the fuels, raw materials, and
markets of the world. Our armies have proved themselves to be
a necessary evil in a world that has never accepted the Buddhism of Buddha or the Christianity of Christ. Governments
content that they must not be deterred from war by the Ten
Commandments, or the reluctance of the young to be killed, or
of older men to be taxed, say they must think not of present
feelings only but of future perspectives and results. Who can
tell what our grandchildren will wish that we had done today?
They, too, should be counted in our polls.

So the Pentagon claims that to protect us from attack or
subversion, from perils present or potential, it must subordinate half of our industry, our science, our universities, and our
taxes to the business of developing and producing the latest and
most deadly weapons, and for teaching ten million youngsters
to kill without moral or religious qualms.

Individuals lust for freedom, goods, and power, and our
governments are ourselves and our desires multiplied, ungov-
erned, and armed. War is the Darwinism or natural selection
of states, and not all our tears will wash it out of history until
the people and governments of the world agree, or are forced,
to yield their sovereignties to some superstate; and then there
will be revolutions and civil wars. For a while we hoped that
our progress from TNT to the hydrogen bomb would deter
men from waging war, but then history asked, "Did the progress from bows and arrows to Big Berthas and lethal rockets

diminish war or extend and intensify it?" Apparently our generation will be spared that holocaust; but who can tell if statesmanship will overcome hatred when Americans tired of war face eight hundred million Chinese remembering a century of white oppression and a decade of American hostility and scorn?

THE PASSING OF CIVILIZATION

And so we come to the final chapter, which is death—not only of the individual but, sooner or later, of our civilization and ultimately of the race. Every life, every society, every species is an experiment, and must give way. The philosopher/historian adjusts himself to this kaleidoscope and does not despair because his children will succeed him, and young civilizations will milk and supplant the old. Civilizations are the generations of the racial soul, which may, through death, give new youth to an ancient heritage. In the train of life it is the old who yield their seats to the young.

SUGGESTIONS

Can we improve our heritage before we pass it on? You have a right to ask me what I would recommend for the betterment of American life. I would make parentage a privilege and not a right. No one has a right to bring a child into the community without having passed tests of physical and mental fitness to breed. To parents who have passed such tests the government should offer an annuity or a tax exemption, for the first eigh-teen years of the first and second child born to them in lawful marriage, but not for any further child. Contraceptive informa-tion and devices should be made available to all married per-sons at minimum cost. The unity of the family and the authority of the parents should be strengthened by making parents legally responsible for their dependent children of minor age and by making the earnings of such children subject to parental control.

Education should be provided to fit every high school grad-uate for practical employment in a technological economy, but education in the humanities—literature, philosophy, history, and the arts—should be equally stressed for the understanding of values and ends and the intelligent use of leisure. Courses in anatomy, physiology, and hygiene should be required in every year of schooling.

All orderly proposals for high school, college, or university reform should be submitted to a board of which the elected president of each class should be a voting member. Administra-tors should dismiss any student who has violently interfered with the operation of the school. Students and the public should recognize and protect our universities as the finest insti-tutions in America and the last against which protest should take a violent form, for they and a free press will be our stron-gest defense against dictatorship.

To balance the commercialism and partiality of private broadcasting systems and news media, I would recommend the establishment of a US broadcasting company, financed by the government but controlled by our universities.

I should like every religious institution to preach morality rather than theology, and welcome into its fellowship every person who accepts the Golden Rule and the Ten Commandments as the ideal toward which he strives to grow.

Education in morality—that is, the conscientious cooperation of the individual with the group—should be given in every week of schooling from kindergarten to PhD. In the last two years of high school and in every year of college, detailed instruction should be provided in sex education, and in the effects of sexual promiscuity, narcotics, tobacco, and alcohol. Every high school girl should be instructed in the physical, moral, and social results of extramarital relations; and every youth should be taught his moral obligation to treat every girl as he would like youths to treat his sister.

The reduction of poverty, and the extension of education, will reduce (though they will not end) crime. Temporary insanity should no longer be accepted as an excuse for crime. Prisons should be replaced by well-enclosed state farms, each designed for a separate grade of offender, and all designed by an orderly and open-air life to teach useful occupations and to restore the inmate to the behavior of a responsible citizen.

Every encouragement should be given to the further organization of labor, as a desirable counterpoise to the organization of industrialists, merchants, bankers, and generals. The National Labor Relations Board should act to reduce, or, if possible, end, racial or religious discrimination by admission to union membership or jobs.

The unemployed should be used by federal and state governments in works of social utility and environmental improvement.

A department of consumers' research should be made a well-financed part of the president's cabinet.

Our industrial leaders should welcome and help to implement the welfare state as a humane mitigation of the painful inequality of human fortune, and a saving substitute from social turmoil and dictatorial repression.

I should advise youth to be skeptical of revolution as a monster that devours its own fathers and its children. Less alluring, but less costly, are those processes of reform, by persistent propaganda and gradual implementation, which have achieved so many beneficent changes in our economic and political life in this century. Persons under thirty should never trust the economic, political, or moral ideas of any person under thirty.

Schools of government should be promoted in our universities and prepare college graduates for political administration, and a US civil academy should be established to give the graduates of such schools further instruction in legislation, administration, and diplomacy. Perhaps we can persuade the electorate to prefer such graduates for public office.

Treaties of nonaggression and nonsubversion should be promoted among all major states.

The jurisdiction of the Permanent Court of Arbitration at The Hague should be extended and accepted as fast as the education of citizens and officeholders will permit.

Perhaps through such developments America may liberate itself from domination by men who flourish in war and languish in peace.

I should recommend—though I cannot promise to practice—a peaceful acceptance of death when it comes in due time or by unavoidable fate. I believe a physician should not artificially prolong the life of a person whom three physicians have pronounced to be immediately near death; I hereby consent to such an abbreviation of my vegetable days.

CONCLUSION

As I think back upon this discourse, I fear that I have stressed too heavily the problems that face us and our children: the stifling of quality with quantity, the breakdown of marriage and the family, the racial disorder in our schools, the loosening of morals, the hopeless ghettos in our cities, the crime in our streets, the corruption in public office, the skepticism of democracy among radicals and reactionaries alike, the erosion of our moral fiber by the brutalities of war. But these are the stark realities that distort broadcast or printed news, that move our sons and daughters to revolt, and ourselves to wonder have we the strength and courage to meet these accumulated ills.

We can meet them only by a resolute act of mutual understanding. We elders must find it in our souls to be patient with our children, to hear them fondly even when they rant, to recognize that their wild intransigence has spurred some remedial action in legislative chambers, and in administrative halls. These youngsters have something to say that needs saying, and that no one else can say. Perhaps our national vitality depends upon a continuing tension between youth and age, whereby innovation meets tradition, and the ardor of experiment fuses with the coolness of experience.

NOTES

CHAPTER SIX: OUR SOULS

1. *New York Times*, June 23, 1934.

2. When, in 1913, I first read the five volumes of Santayana's The Life of Reason, I was thoroughly unconvinced by his denial of any efficacy to thought or consciousness (*Reason in Common Sense*, Chapter IX; *Reason in Science*, Chapter III). "Thought is in no way instrumental. . . . The mind at best vaguely forecasts the result of action; . . . but this premonition . . . can obviously give no aid or direction to the unknown mechanical process that produced it and that must realize its own prophecy, if that prophecy is to be realized at all" (*Reason in Common Sense*, 214). Rereading those chapters after fifty-four years, I still find them unconvincing. That thought and consciousness should have been so laboriously and progressively developed by evolution despite complete lack of influence upon action and life, seems highly impossible in theory, as well as quite contrary to our most direct and frequent experience. But seldom has an incredible philosophy been so graced with style— metaphors flashing light upon abstractions, words molded into hypnotizing music. Read and beware! (Santayana in later years regretted those five volumes, but still called himself a materialist.)

3. *Reason in Religion*, Chapter XIV.

CHAPTER EIGHT: ON RELIGION

1. *New York Times*, April 30, 1967.

CHAPTER NINE: ON A DIFFERENT SECOND ADVENT
1. *Thus Spake Zarathustra*, New York, 1906, 4.
2. *Ecce Homo*, London, 1911, 141.

CHAPTER ELEVEN: ON MORALITY
1. Harold March, *Gide and the Hound of Heaven*, Philadelphia, 1952, 87f.

CHAPTER SEVENTEEN: ON POLITICS
1. Polybius, *The Histories*, III, vi, 5.

CHAPTER TWENTY-TWO: ON THE INSIGHTS OF HISTORY
1. As an example, I would cite John Updike's novel *Couples*.
2. Plato, *The Republic*, 562.

Will Durant (1885–1981) was awarded the Pulitzer Prize (1968) and the Medal of Freedom (1977). He spent more than fifty years writing his critically acclaimed series of books entitled The Story of Civilization (the later volumes written in conjunction with his wife, Ariel) and capped off his magnificent career with *Heroes of History*, written when Durant was ninety-two. His first book, *The Story of Philosophy*, has remained in print for over seven decades and is credited with introducing more people to the subject of philosophy than any other work. Throughout his life, Durant was passionate in his quest to bring philosophy out of the ivory towers of academia and into the lives of everyday men and women. A champion of human rights issues such as the brotherhood of man and social reform long before such issues were popular, Durant, through his writings, continues to entertain and educate readers the world over, inspiring millions of people to lead lives of greater perspective.

INDEX

population growth and,
160
war and quest for, 92, 93,
94
Ford, Henry, 156
Ford, John Anson, 76–77
foreign languages, 147
France, 162
Freud, Sigmund, 49, 73, 135
Frick, Henry Clay, 117

G

Gauss, Karl Friedrich, 37
Geneva Agreements of 1954,
106
Germany, 137–138
Gide, Andre, 73
Goethe, Johann Wolfgang
von, 145
Goldman, Emma, 117
Greece
Greek literature, 148
Greek mythology, 164
Gregory VII, Pope, 50

H

Hague, The, 176
Hall, G. Stanley, 22
happiness, in youth, 17

Heisenberg, Werner, 38
Helmholtz, Hermann von,
40
Henry VIII, 71
history, insights of, 156–158
family, 161–162
human nature, 159
human population,
160–161
morality, 164–167
religion, 163–164
school, 162–163
war, 172–173
work, 167–171
Hitler, Adolf, 97
Ho Chi Minh, 106
Hoover, Herbert, 111
human nature, 159
human population, 160–161
Hume, David, 35, 65

I

Icarus, 31
immigration, 113, 175–176
indeterminacy, principle of,
38
Industrial Revolution, 128
family dynamics and, 161
moral change and, 62–63
warfare and, 95